P9-DWO-003

The Book of Chinese Beliefs

Frena Bloomfield is a British journalist and
broadcaster who now lives and works in
Hong Kong.

Frena Bloomfield

The Book of Chinese Beliefs

A journey into the Chinese inner world

Arrow Books

Arrow Books Limited
17-21 Conway Street, London W1P 6JD

An imprint of the Hutchinson Publishing Group

London Melbourne Sydney Auckland
Johannesburg and agencies throughout
the world

First published 1983
Reprinted 1985

© Frena Bloomfield 1983

This book is sold subject to the condition that it
shall not, by way of trade or otherwise, be lent,
resold, hired out, or otherwise circulated
without the publisher's prior consent in any
form of binding or cover other than that in
which it is published and without a similar
condition including this condition being imposed
on the subsequent purchaser

Printed and bound in Great Britain by
Anchor Brendon Limited, Tiptree, Essex

ISBN 0 09 931900 4

This book is offered with the greatest respect to Dr Lam and Dr Butt from a very humble pupil.

It is dedicated with great affection to Evelyn Lambert who is not only *une grande dame* but also a great dame.

Acknowledgements

I wish to express my very grateful thanks to the following people: Dan and SuJen Rocovits, whose deep knowledge of Taiwan and painstaking research on my behalf have greatly contributed to the factual contents of this book; the Hong Kong Tourist Association, for ungrudging help and the use of its library, with special mention to Wendy, Vivien and Terry, among others; Robin Hutcheon, Managing Editor of the *South China Morning Post*, for allowing me to quote from his newspaper; and my long-suffering and patient friends and advisers: Gary Butt, Mo-ling Leong, Willie Mark, Alice Yao and Timothy Yau.

Thanks too to J. Dean Barrett for permitting me to use material from my former book, *The Occult World of Hong Kong*, published in 1981 in Hong Kong by Hong Kong Publishing.

Contents

1. The Invisible People

The Chinese outnumber everyone else on this planet and they are also the most widely distributed ethnic group on earth, but they are perhaps among the least-known and least-understood people in the world too. Some of this is undoubtedly due to their innate sense of privacy and a certain reluctance to let themselves be known by strangers, in addition to the position of the modern Chinese in China who have been secluded behind a bamboo curtain of political isolation which is only now beginning to be drawn aside. However, a much more cogent reason for this is the fact that most non-Chinese have not stopped to look at all closely at the Chinese around them. Anthropologists do study Chinese society but then they share their knowledge largely with other members of the academic community. Political students look at Singapore, Hong Kong, China and Taiwan and speculate about the future of these nations and colonies. Classical Chinese scholars immerse themselves in the writings of the long-dead poets of the Golden Age or consider the works of

Confucius. The harsh fact is that all these careful studies have as much to do with the average life of a Chinese as the study of Shakespeare does with the life of a Yorkshire miner. The ordinary Chinese seem to be too ordinary, too unclassical and too unexciting to rate much attention and consequently the rest of the world is as ignorant of the waiters who serve their food in Chinese restaurants or of the student studying mathematics at university as they are of the life of extraterrestrials.

This book explores the world of the ordinary Chinese; those who pass so quietly among strangers in the streets of New York, San Francisco, Vancouver, London and cities the whole world over; those who throng so noisily amid the safety of their own people in Hong Kong, Taiwan and Singapore. It does not pretend to be exhaustive, but it is an introduction to the life style and beliefs – social and religious – which the Chinese have taken with them all over the world. Not for nothing have the Chinese remained a race apart, for they are one of the few ethnic groups who have preserved the traditions and beliefs of thousands of years and yet have, at the same time, adapted to the computer age.

The Chinese are a group beset by legends, mysteries and long-standing traditional lore. Some of it we cannot explain by anything in western knowledge and some of it we might regard as mere superstition. Certain aspects of Chinese beliefs have already been proven according to the scientific standards which are so important to the West, while others remain untested or in the process of being tested. Whichever heading it comes under, most Chinese lore is fascinating and some of it controversial. Often, we find that the Chinese themselves do not know what lies behind the behaviour and habits established by centuries as they have maintained the life style but not the learning which explains it.

Wherever they go the Chinese carry their habits with them and they tend to preserve them to a greater or lesser extent. Whether they live in China itself, in Chinese communities or as an alien group in a largely Caucasian society, they do not vary as much as outsiders might expect them to. They certainly do not solicit attention from strangers. In fact, they much prefer to remain private and withdrawn as a community, meeting official faces with a blank stare or muttered incomprehension. Nevertheless, conversely, they also appreciate a genuine interest in their traditions and an understanding of their lore.

The ordinary Chinese are not those concerned with Confucius or the mysteries of Taoism, even though both names will be much vaunted in public. Confucius may be read from beginning to end and you will still know very little about what makes the normal street-level Chinese community operate, especially when it comes down to traditional obligations, beliefs, superstitions and even etiquette. To know about those things, you have to live among such a community, be observant and ask plenty of questions. It is often said that such traditions are secret and that the Chinese are reluctant to talk about them. There are, of course, hidden aspects of belief, but in general the Chinese are willing enough to talk to those who want to understand them.

There are many beliefs which influence daily life in Chinese communities. Some deal with religious duties or with the mysteries of fortune, others deal with matters which outsiders might think of as superstition which have no factual basis. Set aside the words of Confucius and the philosophy of Taoism and it becomes clear that the real religion of the ordinary Chinese is involved with the pursuit of worldly success, the appeasement of the dead and the spirits and the seeking of hidden knowledge about the future. All of this is controlled, so the Chinese believe, by paying ritualistic respect to the dead to keep their spirits quiet and satisfied, by seeking harmony in everyday life and by using various methods of divination. It is around these concerns that Chinese community life is built and it is these customs which the Chinese have carried all over the world with them, even into the sophisticated United States and Canada.

It is these customs also which seem most mysterious to outsiders, either because they have never seen them or because, having observed them, they do not understand what they represent. It is also about these matters that the Chinese are reluctant to speak to outsiders, fearing ridicule or merely wishing to appear thoroughly modern and free of attitudes which might seem primitive to others. This is particularly true of those who have been educated in the West or those who come from the upper strata of Chinese society, who have always been less involved with the peasant crudities of the vast majority of the Chinese people.

Apart from the seeking of good fortune, the major aim of the Chinese is to keep their relationship with the dead as smooth and happy as possible. The Chinese, more than any other people, are obsessed with the dead. Ancestor worship is often described by the more sophisticated Chinese as respect for the dead, a living symbol of the Chinese love of continuing tradition. In fact, for the average Chinese, ancestor worship indicates a fear of the dead – the terror that the spirits of the dead will come back to bring harm to the living if they are not placated by constant care and attention. Filial respect may well be involved in this, but the bottom line is fear. Fear is also a recurrent theme in Chinese dealings with the spirits, not only spirits of the dead but also the spirits of place or nature that are wandering around the world and sometimes encounter human beings on their journeying. These spirits too have to be respected and cared for, in case they take vengeance on human beings who annoy them.

When we examine these matters in the course of this book, we are looking at what happens now in Chinese communities all over the world, including Communist China. Although these attitudes have a lengthy history stretching back thousands of years, they are also still relevant and still affect daily life, even in the most apparently modern Chinese societies, as examples will demonstrate. It is this direct connection between past and present which makes Chinese society unique. It is undoubtedly this which has enabled the Chinese to keep their ethnic identity so strong and so individual in a world where homogeneity is the rule.

Those who want to plumb the deepest mysteries of Chinese life and customs may begin here, but they will have to turn to scholars and anthropologists to learn more. This book is mean to be a signpost along the way, an introduction to this profoundly separate people whom most of the world know only by their cooking styles, their laundries and their tailoring. At least this book will get you past those superficial clichés without drowning you in the classical seas where most Chinese in fact never set sail themselves.

2. Fung shui:
Chinese earth magic

'Did bad *fung shui* kill Bruce Lee?' demanded a Hong Kong newspaper headline, one week after the world's most famous kung fu fighter died suddenly at the age of thirty-two. While the question might be meaningless to many, it is instantly comprehensible to any Chinese throughout the world and also to anyone in contact with a Chinese community, whether it be in Singapore, Hong Kong or London. No one lives in such places for long without hearing the phrase *fung shui* (also commonly spelt *feng shui*), although it takes somewhat longer to understand what it means. In fact, according to *fung shui* professors, it takes a lifetime of study to comprehend its complexities.

The Cantonese phrase *fung shui* means 'wind and water', though that does little to explain it, and the wide variety of situations in which the phrase is used only confuses the issue further. It might be a house left standing empty for no apparent reason. 'Bad *fung shui*,' say the neighbours and nobody will live there, no matter how high the demand for housing. A young business-man returned to Singapore from Harvard opens his computer agency on a date picked for him by a *fung shui* professor as being especially auspicious. An old man dies and his family consults a *fung shui* expert to pick the best burial site. Read a newspaper in any Chinese community and the chances are high that every day there will be a news story concerning *fung shui*.

Two recent stories in Hong Kong, very different from each other in their content, illustrate this. 'Bank Shifts the Big Cats', says a headline in the *South China Morning Post* of 20 June 1981, and the first paragraph reads: 'Under the watchful eye of a *fung shui* man, the Hong Kong and Shanghai Bank's famous bronze lions were moved at dawn yesterday as a prelude to the bank's redevelopment of its headquarters.'

The other story, from the *Star* newspaper of 14 June 1982, is headlined: 'Meifoo Chimney Cops the Blame', and introduces a tragic incident which begins: 'Last week's Unchau kindergarten bloodbath, in which four children were slain and thirty others injured, was the result of bad *fung shui*. That's the finding of *fung shui* expert Tam Chin-kin who was hired by the kindergarten to see how it could avoid such incidents in the future.' The story went on to explain that the industrial chimney opposite the kindergarten, which had been the scene of a violent rampage by a mentally sick man, resembled the incense sticks burned at funerals and therefore brought back luck to the kindergarten.

All of which sounds both vague and yet complex, involved and yet primitively superstitious. Just what is the truth of Chinese belief about *fung shui* and anyway, what is it? Well, the answer is indeed complex and understanding *fung shui* is complicated even more by the fact that in most Chinese societies it has become very debased by the addition of local folk-myth and by its use as a sort of good-luck insurance system by those who think they know about it but actually do not. However, the inner tradition of *fung shui* is a continuance of a long-standing classical Chinese world system.

At the start, it looks like a simple though bizarre system whereby it is assumed that there is a certain balance in the world and that by a certain set of actions a man may insure the greatest possible benefit for himself. In reality, of course, there is far more to it. The belief is a fundamental one which operated all over China, and probably still does. Any understanding of it must be based upon the traditional scholar's metaphysical viewpoint.

One of the few books ever to have been written about the subject in English is the Rev. E. J. Eitel's *Feng Shui*, published in 1873. Mr Eitel was a long-term resident of Hong Kong who also travelled in China and had as good a comprehension of the belief as any westerner is likely to get.

To quote:

[the Chinese] look upon nature not as a dead inanimate fabric, but as a living breathing organism. They see a golden chain of spiritual life running every form of existence and binding together, as in one living body, everything that subsists on heaven above or on earth below . . .

The whole system of *fung shui* is based upon this emotional concept of nature.

Interestingly enough, the modern view of physics would probably come to meet the boundaries of the Chinese view of nature and the world much more closely than Mr Eitel ever dreamed possible in his somewhat complacent Victorian certitude that he knew much of the truth of the essential nature of things.

Fung shui as it is accepted today is actually quite a modern system. It is based upon the ancient classics but it was formulated and systemized by Wang Chi and other Sung dynasty scholars (1126 – 1278 AD). According to these scholars, there was believed to be one abstract principle in the beginning which was the first cause of all existence. When it first moved, its breath produced the great male principle (*yang*) and when it rested it produced the female principle (*yin*). The energy vitalizing these two principles is *ch'i*, or the breath of nature. As this breath, *ch'i*, went forth, producing the first male and female principles, then gradually the whole universe and everything in it, it was all done according to fixed and immutable laws known as *li*. All these laws were observed by the ancients to be working according to strict mathematical principles which dominated the universe, called *so*. The workings of these three – the *ch'i* (breath), *li* (laws) and *so* (mathematical principles) – are not discernible to ordinary men. They appear subtly in the phenomena of nature and the outward forms of the physical world, known as *ying*. These four divisions (*ch'i, li, so* and *ying*) constitute the theoretical system of *fung shui*.

Although all this sounds somewhat abstract, the actual application of *fung shui* throughout Chinese history has been extremely practical. Early writings mention that government buildings were constructed on the principles suggested by *fung shui* experts called in for their expertise, and all the ancient palaces and temples were built strictly in accordance with the same rules. Even today, in Taiwan, Hong Kong and Singapore, most modern developments have their *fung shui* aspects. In Singapore, for example, a block of public housing flats had to be structurally changed because front doors faced each other – a bad *fung shui* aspect – and people were refusing to live in them until the position of the doors was moved. In Hong Kong, when the splendid new Regent Hotel was designed, architects had to make sure that the building did not cut off completely the wide sweep of the harbour which is why the hotel boasts a huge glass atrium through which the harbour is totally visible. This conforms to the demands of good *fung shui*.

When it comes to the *fung shui* guidelines for the siting of buildings and the planning of villages, most people would not find much to argue with, however much they might disagree with the divinatory aspects of *fung shui*. The classics give a splendid recipe for choosing the ideal site – one which anyone can easily appreciate. They say that, when picking a plot, the owner should make sure that it has mountains to the north, to prevent the evil spirits (of the north winds from Mongolia) having undue access to the site. The front of the land should face the warm south and trees should be growing on the north side. Streams should encircle it and there should be a plain lying to the south, 'big enough for 10,000 horses', and there should be river access big enough to float a long boat. From the top of the hill, the view should extend for miles and rivers and streams to water the plain should be numerous. Such a site, say the classicists, 'will result in the birth of many children and grandchildren'.

Anyone who walks around the Imperial City in Peking today will be looking at a fine example of *fung shui* construction on the grandest scale, just as any tourist who goes to Hong Kong's New Territories can see very fine examples of such construction on a more domestic scale. Probably the best is the walled village of Kam Tin, now something of a tourist trap and on nearly all tour group itineraries. However, what most of the tourists do not know, as they walk around this fourteenth-century village, is that the site was chosen for its *fung shui* aspects. The village is inhabited by a single clan, the Tangs. They fled from the warring provinces of China to the comparative pastoral quiet of what is today the still somewhat rural New Territories, and they picked this particular spot because it conformed to the best classical principles. The village lies in a valley surrounded by hills forming a protective armchair shape. The valley is well watered by rivers and streams and within the walls of the village each house has been constructed with inner courtyards like a private mandala containing the heart of the dwelling.

In Singapore all the oldest temples have been built according to these principles. One fine example can be seen in the Giok Hong Tian Temple in Havelock Road. It even boasts an engraved plaque which specifically states that it was built 'in a peaceful and wholesome street' with a green hill behind it and the Singapore river in front, all surrounded by greenery. All the old temples in Singa-

pore have the same hand-picked *fung shui* and each bears
an explanatory plaque which details the geomantic basis
for the construction of the temple on that site.

Despite the formulae of *fung shui*, it is still no easy task
to pick the best site. All the various factors to be
considered tend to be somewhat obscure, and this is
exactly what keeps the *fung shui* professor in business.
Part of the geomancer's art – or science – is to be able to
balance up all the possible influences of a place. Even so,
none of the aspects are immutable and this is made
obvious by the fact that during Imperial times it was
possible for one litigant to sue another for infringing on
his good *fung shui*. Each complainant would have his own
geomantic expert who would argue the merits of the case
before a judge who would finally give judgement to the
one who made out the best case.

Fung shui is no longer recognized as a viable part of
most legal processes, even among the totally Chinese
communities of the world. However, interestingly
enough, in the British colony of Hong Kong which is, of
course, subject to British law, literally millions of dollars
have been paid out in compensation to people who claim
that their good *fung shui* has been damaged by government building, construction and land development pro-
jects. Such payments have encouraged certain witnesses
of all this to be somewhat cynical about whether the
belief in *fung shui* is genuine or merely a device to squeeze
money out of a nervous colonial government.

This is not a new problem for colonial governments
dealing with a Chinese population. The Rev. E.J. Eitel in
his book *Feng Shui*, mentioned above, has the following
tale to tell.

When Senhor Amaral, the Governor of Macao, who combined
with a great passion for constructing roads an unlimited
contempt for *Feng shui*, interfered with the situation and aspects
of Chinese tombs, he was waylaid by Chinese, his head cut off,
and the Chinese called this dastardly deed the revenge of *Feng
shui*.

Usually this kind of offence these days does not result in the cutting off of offending heads in Hong Kong, but it can still cost a lot of money. The Imperial authorities certainly recognized the advantages of interfering with good *fung shui* when the situation seemed to demand it. Whenever a rebellion broke out against Imperial power, one of the first actions of the Emperor was to send messengers to find out who the leaders were and then to trace their ancestral tombs. These were then broken into, their contents scattered and the graves totally desecrated. This had the double role of disheartening the rebels and ensuring the downfall of their family, not only for the present generation but for all future ones as well.

This flexibility of *fung shui* is part of its mystery. It is accepted as being an amoral force and anyone may profit from its good aspects, whether he deserves to or not. *Fung shui* experts are consequently very fussy about who they work for and reluctant to do anything for strangers of whose moral conduct they know nothing. They prefer to keep their arts for the deserving, though at the price a good geomancer commands these days, there must surely be some doubt that this still applies.

Although the many theories of *fung shui* are much bruited about in Chinese communities, they are not necessarily understood by most people. The general use of *Bhat Gwa* mirrors all over Hong Kong is a good example of this. These little hexagonal mirrors can be seen everywhere: in windows, opposite doors, in shops, temples and scattered somewhat randomly around most homes. These are *fung shui* mirrors which are supposed to reflect bad *fung shui* back to where it came from. One well-known example of the use of such mirrors is to be found as the result of the bad *fung shui* of the American Consulate. For the last few years, since the major terrorist scares in the world, the building has had special mirror glass in its windows. The reflections cast back by these windows face directly into the Hong Kong Government's legal department and all the way along the legal department windows these *Bhat Gwa* mirrors can be seen, directing the bad *fung shui* reflection from the Consulate. This is a result of the arbitrary decision of clerks in the legal department; it is very doubtful that there is actually anything wrong with the American Consulate windows in *fung shui* terms.

It was, in fact, one of these *Bhat Gwa* mirrors that indirectly led to the death of Bruce Lee, with which this chapter started. Lee's Chinese nickname was Siu Lung or the Little Dragon. Once he had made his film fortune, he decided to buy a villa in the fashionable area of Kowloon known as Kowloon Tong. The whole area, though popular among rich young Chinese, tends to be left alone by the traditional older Chinese because of its bad *fung shui*. This results largely from the fact that it lies in a valley and all valleys have bad *fung shui*. Knowing this, Lee called in a geomancer who placed a *Bhat Gwa* mirror on a tree outside his house to improve the *fung shui*. However, just before he died, a great typhoon blew down the tree and broke the mirror, leaving Lee unprotected. This was the chance the evil elements had been waiting for. Not for nothing is Kowloon called Kowloon, which means Nine Dragons. The Nine Dragons, jealous of the challenge presented to them by the Little Dragon, struck back at Lee while he was unprotected and so he suddenly died at a tragically early age and at the height of his success. It is not necessary to be physically in the place of bad *fung shui* to suffer its effects. They can and do carry over into life in general.

It is to offset the long-term and long-range effects of bad *fung shui* that good grave sites are chosen. Of course, it takes an expert to pick the site and even to pick the day on which excavation can begin. To disturb the earth in any way, either by building on it or by digging into it, is to run serious risk of being affected by bad *fung shui*. The task of the *fung shui* expert is to ensure that such action does not bring about misfortune. To this end, he comes along with his books and with the geomantic instruments of his trade and sets his scholarship to work to site the grave adequately. The value of a good resting place is not taken lightly by the Chinese and, once they have found one, they do not relinquish it easily.

Many of the families who now live in Hong Kong originally came from China where their ancestral graves are. Since the Chinese Communist takeover of 1949, it has not been possible for those who die in Hong Kong to be transported back to the family resting place in China. Rather than ever give up hoping that they will one day lie in the ancestral resting place, the families compromise with an arrangement that might seem bizarre to others, but which makes perfect sense to them. They put their dead to rest in a temporary hostel where they lie, attended by an old man who makes offerings and burns incense for the spirits of the dead, until the day of their return to China. The house of the dead is run by one of the biggest hospital groups in Hong Kong, the Tung Wah Group, and the residents of the hostel have a small monthly rental paid for them by their families. They lie either in dormitories or alone, but men and women are never put together unless they are married to each other and, when you recall that the Chinese believe in all kinds of activities for the dead, that makes sense. It is said that one of Hong Kong's richest millionaires keeps his mother's body there, waiting for the day when he can send her back to her ancestral resting place in China.

This is done to keep the effects of good *fung shui* in the family. It is believed that a family's fortune has a lot to do with the siting of its graves. Therefore, particularly if a family has become successful (which demonstrates the power of the good *fung shui* from the graves), they are all the more keen to maintain such benevolent influences. After Doctor Sun Yat-sen became the first President of the Republic of China, other ambitious people started sneaking their own family graves nearer and nearer that of his mother, hoping that some of the good *fung shui* which had made her son a new emperor would somehow carry over into their own family fortunes.

While many people might see the *fung shui* principles of good building as being quite sensible, though exotically expressed, most non-Chinese find it difficult to accept that the siting of someone else's grave can possibly affect anything to do with the living. It is even harder for non-Chinese to understand and accept some of the more esoteric tales of good and bad *fung shui*.

Another headline: 'Police Killing: Families Blame Church for Bad *Fung Shui*'. The residents of a police married quarters were blaming the pointed roof and huge concrete cross of a church opposite their building for projecting bad *fung shui* on them. This, they claimed, was what caused the death of Police Sergeant Tse Yun-cheung. The more immediate and apparent cause of death was that the sergeant was gunned down during a bank robbery.

Yet one more headline: 'Bad *Fung Shui* Haunts Radio Station'. Two deaths had occurred at the Radio Television Hong Kong studio and the employees were claiming it was because the studio was built over the mass grave of people killed during the Japanese occupation. Later on, the main gate of the radio station was closed, as it remains to this day, in order to set the bad *fung shui* to rights. Anyone who goes to Radio Hong Kong's Kowloon studio will have to pick his way awkwardly round to get to the front door as the entrance now remains unusable.

The story does not stop there. It is not uncommon to find a completely mixed metaphor operating in the case of some *fung shui* stories. An interesting example occurred in the rural New Territories in recent years. Two villages situated very near each other had long followed very different destinies; one was rich while the other was poor. The poor villagers eventually called in a *fung shui* expert and asked him what they could do to improve their fortunes. After duly considering their state, he came out with the following explanation for their plight.

'You see,' he explained, 'all you people are called Ng.'

(It is not uncommon in the New Territories for a whole village to be of one clan.)

'Now, as you all know, Ng means "fish". Now that village over there, if you look carefully, is built in the shape of a fish-net. And that's what's happening to all your good fortune. That fish-net is catching all you fish people and stealing your fortunes from you. You will never be prosperous as long as you live here.'

So all the tribe of fish people packed up and moved away. Unfortunately, history does not record whether or not their luck changed for the better.

This kind of poetic imagery often appears in matters of *fung shui*. One famous example quoted by Sinologist Maurice Freedman is this: 'The great pagoda on An-ching, the port in Anhwei Province, is said to function as a mast for the port, which is said to resemble a junk. Two enormous anchors hang on the pagoda's walls, their original purpose having been to prevent the city drifting away downstream.'

There are different schools of *fung shui*, each with an emphasis on something considered to be of special significance. For example, the Fukien school places major importance on the use of certain instruments, while the Kiangsi school stresses the importance of the formation of landscapes and their resemblance to certain animals, actual or mythical. This school, also known as the School of Forms, is the one which dominates Hong Kong, though the two schools have tended to fuse since the nineteenth century.

A Hong Kong geomancer will therefore pay great attention to landscape and when siting a house for a client, for example, will be sure to avoid building it upon a dragon's tail, or some other more sensitive part of its anatomy. Any hill, however small, is thought to be a dragon and houses sited foolishly will fall when the disturbed dragon begins to flick its tail angrily. Actually, given that China is a land subject to sudden and devastating earthquakes, it does not take a very poetic imagination to see an earth tremor as the angry thrashing of a subterranean dragon's tail. When construction workers digging out a site come across the rich red soil which marks a high iron ore content, they usually become very agitated. The red, they say, is the dragon's blood which has been spilled by their digging and they will normally refuse to continue working on such a site, at least until the geomancer comes to set things right.

It is considered essential among the Chinese construction workers of Singapore, Hong Kong and Taiwan that all the proper observances are made. Without them, the workers would simply refuse to continue. Even the most modern developer does nothing until the *fung shui* man has been called in to do his job and, if it is not the *fung shui* man, then it must be the Taoist priests who know how to deal with spirits which would otherwise create trouble. Thus, the huge multi-million-dollar Mass Transit Railway project, which gave Hong Kong the biggest modern underground railway in the world, started with an invocation given by a whole bank of Taoist priests. They paid respects to all the spirits of the earth who were about to be outraged by having their domain violated.

The geomancer stands somewhere between the scholars of ancient China and the common people, and is greatly respected for his knowledge. A typical example of such a man is Lau Chi-leung, a well-known geomancer who lives in a smart new villa in Tai Po, a market town in Hong Kong's New Territories.

Mr Lau is a slightly-built man in his fifties. He has a gentle, almost humble, manner and he delights in sharing his knowledge with those who seek it from him. In fact, it is one of his causes for regret that he has no apprentice to train.

'My father was himself a scholar of *fung shui*,' he says proudly. 'He went to Kiangsi itself, to study at the famous school there. And he learned many things and when it was time he returned to Hong Kong and when I was old enough to begin, he taught me what he knew.' This is the normal way in which this knowledge is passed from one practitioner to another.

At fifty-five, Mr Lau says he is still learning and expects to do so until his death.

'Women make very good geomancers. In fact, they tend to be far better than men. It's because they're much better at fine detail and they work from a sense of intuition which isn't so developed in men. My own father studied with a very famous woman philosopher. I'm sorry to say there are no women in Hong Kong with these skills now. It's very sad. There aren't many young people coming into this profession of ours either. I don't know of anyone under the age of thirty studying it. Probably because the results are invisible and, of course, it takes a long time to complete the studies too.'

Mr Lau stands outside his villa. It is a finely built house, in traditional Chinese style, soaring eaves edged with porcelain tiles, ornately decorated as dragons, phoenixes and lions. There are plants and well-established trees around and he gazes out at the view, picked – naturally – for its fine *fung shui*.

'There, you see, now I'll show you what good *fung shui* looks like in a landscape. This house sits right here between the gentle curve of those two hills opposite. The peak of the third faces it directly and this is an ideal site to get the best of the aspects. There's only one problem and that isn't in the landscape. Come, I'll show you.'

Just opposite we can see the pointed eaves of a neighbouring house, threateningly angled towards him.

'Now that is bad *fung shui*. To offset that, I placed a *Bhat Gwa* (eight-sided mirror) on my roof and that deflects any bad influences.' He gives a sigh and shakes his head. 'You know, you can look around anywhere in Hong Kong and see those mirrors. People just don't know how to use these things so they just seem to put as many around them as they can, without the slightest idea of what they're doing.'

Mr Lau works full-time as a geomancer, and his clients include the entire village of Shung Shui, a small New Territories village. The village headman was actually sitting in his villa when we arrived to talk to Mr Lau and as he spoke he turned to the man for confirmation.

His telephone rings the whole time we are talking with him. Consultations, advice, admonitions. This is typical of the kind of demands made on the time of a geomancer.

They are called out whenever they are needed. Some of the best in Taiwan and Hong Kong have even been summoned to the United States for special consultations, at not much less than ten thousand American dollars a time.

'Once the District Office called me in. They'd been having this problem, you know, people getting sick all the time. I had to move all the furniture around for them, but it's okay now. No more sickness.'

Did he advertise? I ask him. He raises his eyebrows and says with gentle reproach: 'To advertise wouldn't be at all professional. People speak for a good geomancer. He needn't speak for himself.'

He gets out the tools which are the mark of his peculiar trade. The geomantic compass consists of a wooden or clay disc, about six inches in diameter with a magnetic compass in the centre. The disc is coated with yellow lacquer and is inscribed with concentric circles. It serves as a model of the universe and Chinese characters are written all over it.

'This was my father's compass. We use it to bring the features of heaven and earth together at a particular site. Then from that we can made suitable predictions and recommendations. When I do that, I make full use of all my books too. These are what I need. Manuals for interpreting the shapes of the physical features of the world. Almanacs for working out the positions of the constellations, for the stars too affect the state of this earth. And we use the *Book of Changes* too, the *I-Ching*.'

The geomancer will often be called in to carry out exorcisms, although strictly speaking, in the old days this was a function of the priests alone. The government itself has been known, somewhat shame-facedly, to call in a geomancer for this purpose. A few years ago, the Government's Public Works Department building was commonly rumoured to be haunted. Those who worked there talked of desks moving around by themselves and strange ghostly figures that were seen after dark. True or not, after a while the civil servants who worked there were refusing to do any overtime which might keep them there after darkness fell. The building, they said, was haunted by the spirits of those who were murdered there by the notorious Japanese secret police during the war. A geomancer was called in; he carried out an exorcism and the ghosts were never seen again.

Another geomancer, Hong Kong's best-known, Choi Park-lai, also comes from a family with a tradition of studying *fung shui*. His grandfather, who was a highly placed civil servant under the Ch'ing dynasty, became intrigued by the study of geomancy. He and a group of friends worked on their discoveries together. His particular ability was for mathematics and he enjoyed the exacting figure work of *fung shui*. He passed his learning to his son who in turn taught his son. Now Mr Choi has a son who is working together with him as a geomancer – the fourth generation. Mr Choi follows the fused Kiangsi and Fukien schools: he explains that, when making *fung shui* judgements, the two most important things are environment plus the figure-work.

A geomancer will also consider colours when he is advising a householder on how and where to build his house. Certain colours are thought to be associated with desirable or unfortunate ideas. For example, grey and black are colours which represent disaster and grief. Green signifies harmony, while yellow and gold mean heavenly glory. The orange and red range are the colours of joy and festivity, white represents purity and blue the meditation of heaven. In Chinese temples throughout the world the dominant colours are gold and bright red. As a decorating device, these colours were the favourites of the Ching dynasty, which was not known for its tasteful restraint.

When a geomancer begins his studies, which usually cannot be before the age of eighteen, he will study the methods of the two schools of *fung shui* which have existed since Sung times. The Fukien school is also known as the Ancestral Hall or Direction Method, and lays more emphasis upon the relationship of the planets and the hexagrams of the *I-Ching*, or *Book of Changes*. The other, the Kiangsi school, which Mr Lau studied, is also called the School of Forms and places emphasis on the formation of the landscape and its relationship with the cosmic breath, or *ch'i*. It is this school which tends to dominate Cantonese society and it looks for animals – mythical or real – in the surrounding landscape. For example, hills or raised ground are considered to be dragons, which are associated with *yang*, heaven, vigour and the colour azure. As we have seen, the name Kowloon means 'Nine Dragons'. It comes from the Cantonese *gau loong* – *gau* is nine and *loong* is dragon. The name came about in this way. The district which is now Kowloon is built upon a range of eight hills. A boy Emperor who lived there remarked upon this to a courtier.

'I see eight dragons round us.'

'But there are nine dragons here,' answered the courtier with the greatest respect.

'Nine?' said the young Emperor. 'How is that?'

'Why you yourself are the ninth!' said the courtier, recalling the convention that a dragon also represented imperial power.

And, from then on, the place was known as Nine Dragons or Kowloon.

In contrast, lowland areas and valleys are said to be tigers, associated with *yin*, earth, quiescence and the colour orange. They very often have bad *fung shui* and certainly in Hong Kong for many years the Chinese refused to live in some of the valley areas, notably Happy Valley which is now where the island's race course is. Bearing in mind that until the second half of the twentieth century it was an area prey to a particular breed of mosquitoes which carried a fatal form of malaria, such a prejudice was very well founded indeed, as is often the case with the apparently random decisions of *fung shui*.

As well as studying the landscape, the geomancer will also be well versed in the classics of *fung shui* and his home library is likely to include copies of *The Imperial Encyclo-*

paedia, written in 1726; *The Water Dragon Classic*, written in 600 AD; Kuo P'u's *Song of Geomancy*, dating from the fourth century BC, as well as other classical writings on the subject. But the major work which he will always carry with him on his rounds is the *I-Ching*, or *Book of Changes*, that same Chinese classic which has become such a popular work of divination for westerners in the last two decades. As a very rough guide, the geomancer uses each trigram to represent a direction of the compass.

☰	= north-west	☶	= north-east
☷	= south-west	☴	= south-east
☳	= east	☲	= south
☵	= north	☱	= west

For the geomancer, the trigrams are all related to the Five Elements and various animals and seasons of the year, and all of this comes together with the one essential tool of the *fung shui* expert, the geomantic compass or *lopan*. The compass was originally invented by the Chinese who then proceeded to use it, not for navigation or travel, but for the purpose of *fung shui*. The name *lopan* literally means reticulated plate. It is a circular instrument inscribed with a number of concentric circles, which can vary from as few as five up to thirty-four, and at its centre is a compass needle. The geomancer uses this to divine the harmonies and suitabilities of sites.

In spite of all this scholastic and esoteric application, it must be said that many of the judgements of *fung shui* are open to argument. It can take two to three generations before the effects of good *fung shui* improve a family's fortunes and the cynical will no doubt not be above observing that this certainly safeguards the geomancer from customer complaints. The variability of *fung shui* also means that, if the first geomancer called on does not achieve the desired results, then a second one is likely to be summoned to look for omissions and set them to rights.

This story from Taiwan is a true tale of *fung shui* in action, as told by American researcher and Chinese-speaker Dan Rocovits.

The Huang family had been warned not to buy a particular piece of land. People said it had very bad *fung shui* (usually spelt *fung swei* in Taiwan). But Mr Huang, the head of the family, was an educated man and didn't believe in *fung shui*. The land was cheap and he bought it. The family then worked very hard to prepare the land for sugar cane planting. Nine months later, poor Mr Huang vomited blood and died and everybody said it was because he hadn't listened to their advice.

The widow sold the land and moved her five young children back to their old home and they were all very poor. The rest of the family looked down on them. Eventually, the widow's eldest son married and he and his new wife moved into a house of their own. They moved into it before it was really completed and they had to board up the openings which were there for the doors and windows. The new bride had a strange dream that night. She dreamed that a great storm blew up and threw the boards back into the house. In the gaping doorway stood the spectral figure of a man.

'Don't be afraid,' he said to her. 'I've just come to tell you that my home does not shelter me from the wind and the rain. Please ask my second son to move me 180 paces to the left of our old family home. There the *fung shui* is better.' He smiled and then neatly exited the same way he came in. The bride woke up and immediately jumped out of bed to rush over to the family altar, to look at the photographs on it. Sure enough, she recognized her spectral visitor as her father-in-law, Mr Huang. The very next day, the family called in a *fung shui* man and asked him to inspect the family grave site, without telling him why or even mentioning the night-time visitor. The *fung shui* man suggested they would be better to resite the grave a little, and his recommendation fortunately harmonized with the wishes of the deceased Mr Huang. The grave was moved and the restless bones of Mr

Huang were laid to their eternal sleep once more.

'Happily,' adds Rocovits, 'the family fortunes began to improve and now they have become the wealthiest members of all their clan.'

There are many stories told in all Chinese societies which have the same theme and, when a particular family begins to prosper in life, others begin to take a good look at their grave sites, as happened with Sun Yat-sen's mother. There are other slightly more chilling tales to be told as well, one of which took place in New York and involved the film actor Gig Young. Gig Young was a talented actor who somehow never really managed to make it big, but surfaced from relative obscurity in 'They Shoot Horses Don't They?' as the frantic MC of the dance marathon around which the Fonda film was built. He made one of his last films in Hong Kong. It was called 'Game of Death' – ironically enough. During the making of the film, Gig Young became romantically involved with a talented young woman writer called Kim Schmidt, whom he married and took back to the United States with him. The couple were said to have been extremely happy together and welcomed friends from Hong Kong to visit them in their luxury apartment in New York. One such friend was a Chinese woman who knew quite a lot about *fung shui* matters. She wandered around the apartment, admired it but pointed out one particular spot which needed a mirror in order to conform with good *fung shui*. The couple nodded and agreed politely but never did anything about it. Some months later, for reasons which have never become public knowledge, Gig Young went into the bedroom, shot his young wife dead by firing a bullet into the back of her head and then killed himself. If the mirror had been placed as the friend had advised, Young's wife would have seen him coming into the room with the gun and possibly the story would not have ended there.

Despite that last sad tale, the effects of *fung shui* are usually much more debatable. The problem is that, as with most traditional areas of traditional Chinese knowledge, so much has been added over the centuries that the central line of teaching has become blurred by detail. It is especially true in areas where folklore and practice have overlaid a classical system or one based originally on the very esoteric and rarified philosophies of the scholars and mystics. In the world today it is true that most of the overseas Chinese communities consist of people with a peasant/farmer background or of similar education and status. Such people are unlikely to have had much to do with the classical knowledge of China and therefore their beliefs and behaviour are largely inherited from their own forebears and are not usually very tightly linked to those of the Mandarin class of scholars or officials. That is why the Chinese can argue endlessly about what exactly makes good *fung shui* and what does not, although they can usually come to a few basic agreements. Ant that, of course, is undoubtedly what keeps *fung shui* experts in business.

It is questionable how much westerners should apply the vocabulary of their own society to the situations of other societies which hold a different system of belief. Sometimes it can help to increase understanding, but it can also merely confuse everyone because the separate vocabularies simply do not fit together. In considering *fung shui*, it is easy enough to agree with the basic architectural principles. It may also be possible to make out a good case for the more mystical side of *fung shui* in that most western psychologists would agree that people's outlook can be made more optimistic or pessimistic by their own actions. One kind of action much touted these days is that of taking charge of one's own life and accepting responsibility. When a family or a community calls in the *fung shui* man to reveal the causes of their bad fortune, they are effectively asking him to show them how to take charge of their own fortunes. By following the guidance he gives them, they expect their outlook to improve and perhaps this optimism and expectation alone gives the necessary boost to enable them to change their own fortunes. That is one possible way for the very sceptical to understand the influence and importance of *fung shui* and the way in which it changes lives.

Those who take an interest in the ancient pathways of the West – the ley lines – may well be able to find many parallels between the Chinese *fung shui* beliefs and those of the leys. This kind of equivalence can be found throughout all study of Chinese culture. It is not a separate culture which has developed quite apart from those of the rest of the world – although this is an idea often fostered by the Chinese themselves, who rarely undertake studies of other cultures, and some Chinese scholars. It is a culture which shares many of its most profound perceptions with other societies, though this might not be immediately apparent.

Interestingly enough, many western architects have been, and are, drawn to the mysteries of *fung shui* through their perception that its principles make a very good basis for town planning. On the grounds that, if the results are impressive then the theories must have some validity, a number have taken up the study of *fung shui*, a study which reveals more secrets the longer it is practised.

3. Gods, ghosts and spirits or what the Chinese really believe

Although the name of Confucius is frequently invoked by Chinese scholars and by the Chinese themselves in most of their public avowals of values, actually there can be no doubt at all that, for the ordinary folk who form the mass of any Chinese community, the real influences are supernatural ones. The Chinese common man has never made the separation of myth and reality that, for example, the westerner has. He has not pushed the supernatural aside, although he may well not speak of it much to strangers and will often refuse to acknowledge its influence. He lives his life with all due deference to the invading presence of the world unseen. He gives the gods their place on his altar, tries to keep the spirits of his ancestors happy lest they return to plague him and avoids, as far as possible, offending the numerous spirits and deities that surround him. Then, if misfortune falls despite all this, he goes to the priest, the medium, the fortune-teller or the diviner and resignedly asks whom he has offended and how he must make amends.

Strangers who live among the Chinese often say they are not religious, merely superstitious, but that is because those strangers do not recognize religion in the form in which the Chinese practise it. Admittedly, it is not the clear-cut philosophical guidance of Confucius, nor the mystic physics of Taoism, with which the common man deals – it is rather the *mélange* of animism, Tao-Buddhist scraps and patches, folk-myth and magic and long centuries of supernatural practices that is now the religion of the Chinese.

Sorting all this out into a single system is confusing, immensely complex and probably just plain impossible. For a start, most Chinese want as little as possible to do with the world of the supernatural – they would much rather leave it all to nuns and monks, diviners, Taoist priests and other specialists, while they themselves get on with the hard enough business of making it in this world. Much of the information going around is entirely contradictory anyway. It is by no means sure that there is an afterlife for the Chinese. Mystical Taoism of the most esoteric kind does not really postulate clear and definite opinions about the shape and form of the afterlife, and popular Taoism – usually referred to by scholars and anthropologists as 'debased' – has so many theories that putting them all together again is like trying to mend Humpty Dumpty. Confucius said nothing about the afterlife but only supported respect for the ancestors and the carrying out of traditional rituals.

Popular beliefs about heaven, hell, the afterlife and the world of the supernatural are, therefore, hard to pinpoint with any real precision as so many variations will be found. A few generalities, however, can be made to help those who want to know the Chinese better at least to make a small start on the task. One thing which will be found in virtually all Chinese households, even in Christian homes, is the family altar.

The family altar is a small shrine, sometimes shaped like a tiny house and hung upon a wall, but most often placed in a position of honour in the main room of the house on the long family table. A variety of deities will be placed on the altar, according to the taste of the family and probably to regional or religious influences. They could, for example, include the Taoist Commanders of the Heavenly Army, the Buddhist *Kwan Yin*, some household gods, the Five Sages and so on. A mixture of religious influences is not at all unusual as the most important factor is that they are Chinese deities and this overrides mere religious differences. This altar will also include the names of the ancestors, certainly of family members recently dead, often together with a photograph of the deceased. In the old days candles were kept burning on the altar, but these have largely been replaced with little red light bulbs. Offerings of burning incense and sometimes fruit and rice grains are also made regularly to the deities of the altar.

Nearly all Chinese shops, businesses, offices and other establishments also have a small altar on display. Even in Britain and the United States, this practice continues. For example, small Chinese takeaways have the deity of the business smiling down on all that chop suey being carried out of the door in little cardboard boxes. Usually the business god will be a minor deity special to that particular trade or profession. Interestingly enough, the virtue of the trade does not seem to affect the issue. Every police station in Hong Kong, for example, has a small shrine with the deity Kwan Tai in it, but then so too do the brothels and the vice dens!

Preferences as to the gods worshipped are entirely personal. It may be that a family has its own special favourite, or that one area has a god considered to be particularly influential. Some people think it wise to spread worship round a bit, so that a wider range of deities can be invoked on special occasions, while other people recommend cultivating one or two gods only and building up a sort of client relationship with them. The choice may also depend upon what has happened in the past. If one god has been useful in previous times of crisis, he is sure to be invoked next time round. If he fails to help, undoubtedly some other deity will do the job instead.

The Chinese in relation to their gods are rather like consumers determined to get the best value for their money. Otherwise they will shop elsewhere. Although the gods, goddesses, sages and others may occupy a position of a certain importance, they certainly do not fill the place of the Christian God, the Jewish Jahweh or the Muslim Allah. Neither do they really have the kind of universal power of, say, the major Hindu deities, like Siva or Kali. They are often seen as powerful but easily led individuals. They can be bribed and they are definitely neither all-knowing nor all-powerful. They are there to be fooled and the Chinese are there to fool them. They have power, perhaps, they get attention, but they do not really win respect and devotion or operate the kind of moral stewardship that the gods of other races and religions do. Often they seem to be downright stupid. Thus, the Kitchen God who usually resides in his own candlelit altar in the house will have his lips smeared with honey on the eve of the Chinese New Year. Tradition says that on that night he will go up to heaven and make a report on the family and the honey is to sweeten what he may say about everyone. This seems to presuppose a certain lack of intelligence, not to say memory, on behalf of the family divinity. Again, in Chinese gangster-style films, the villains often wear hats pulled low over the eyes and dark sunglasses. This is not only a device to fool the law but also to fool the gods so that they will not see their faces and recognize them again.

The gods favoured by a particular family will be seated on the family altar, together with the ancestral tablets. This pattern is common to all Chinese, however irreligious they may be. There are very few Chinese houses or businesses without their altars. Whether people actively believe in the benefits of these divinities is probably debatable, but it is certainly regarded as a form of psychic insurance.

Nevertheless, despite the various sources from which

Chinese religion comes, it is not necessary to see these as separating factors. Just the reverse happens in fact. The Taoist, Buddhist and Confucian elements are regarded by many Chinese as parts of one whole religion. In Hong Kong they use a saying: *San chiao wei yi* ('the three religions are one'). And for most ordinary Chinese, religious life also includes the vast array of local gods, spirits and ghosts which influence everyday life. High-minded scholars and academics from other countries know a lot about Taoism and the works of Confucius, more than most Chinese probably, but they tend to know little about the spiritual beliefs of the greater mass of ordinary working people of fairly low class who make up the bulk of any Chinese population.

And they do have spiritual beliefs. They are passionately involved with the ghosts and spirits of the other world, very aware of the approval or disapproval of the gods as it is manifested in daily life and constantly seeking the voice of the divine in the temples and at home before their own family altars. Their struggle to gain divine favours in various ways is much more intense than the average westerner's involvement with his God.

In village life, in Taiwan and Hong Kong and, to a lesser extent in Singapore, there is a clear structure of divine influences as seen by the Chinese. This becomes rather more obscured in the urbanized Chinese cultures because the relationship with nature tends to become somewhat blurred.

In order of importance, villagers relate to the gods and supernatural beings of Taoism, Buddhism and Confucianism but their choice of favourites varies from place to place. For example, in Hong Kong the favourite choices are the goddess Guan Yin, the god Guan Gong and the goddess Tin Hau. Of these, Guan Yin is considered to be a Buddhist figure, Guan Gong an important Confucian deity and Tin Hau a Taoist goddess.

Although less important in stature, for villagers probably the most significant of their gods are the local deities who are felt to have the most influence over daily life. These would include spirits which inhabited any natural feature of the land which people felt to have a special possessing spirit, such as unusually shaped rocks and boulders or very ancient trees, as well as fields, streams and roads. In Taiwan, for example, it is common for large mango trees, dragon's eye trees – the dragon's eye fruit is a distant cousin of the better known lychee – and large banyans to be the focus for animistic worship of this kind. Most country villages have several such spirits and in Hong Kong the villagers consider that these are usually found in pairs. Various names are given to these spirits, but Hong Kong country folk charmingly call them Bo Gong and Bo Po, which means great-uncles and great-aunts – though part of the friendliness of this name is a sweetener to win the favour of the spirits. On the whole these are thought to be friendly spirits, though they can be nasty if they are not accorded sufficient respect. One tale of retribution comes from Hong Kong. A young boy went out on a school picnic and when he returned home in the evening suddenly developed a very high fever. His mother suspected the hand of spirits in this, as the boy had been completely well that morning when he left for the outing. She questioned him minutely about his activities during the day and managed to extract from him the information that at one point he had stopped to urinate on a tree. Wise countrywoman as she was, she set off to look for this tree and once she found it, she made an offering of joss sticks and rice grains to appease the tree's spirit which had been so insulted by the boy's unthinking action. When she got home, the boy was already feeling better and the fever had broken.

These spirits are generally thought to keep evil ghosts away from a village and they were commonly consulted for aid in times of trouble. To keep them sweet-tempered the villagers usually make offerings during festival times which are much more generous than those made to the run-of-the-mill spirits. The fortunate spirits enjoy a considerable menu of delicacies, such as fish, pork and chicken, as well as candles and joss sticks.

In Taiwan, in addition to rocks, trees and streams, there is a custom of worshipping animals or animal bones. There is one temple where the god of wild cats is worshipped and another temple dedicated to a cat – the Chinese tend to believe that cats are associated with spirits, which gives rise to mixed feelings about them. Some people feel that cats are generally undesirable and the Cantonese in Hong Kong say that a stray cat coming to your house will bring misfortune, while the opposite is true of a stray dog. There is a temple dedicated to a dog god, also in Taiwan, and another temple where the preserved shin bones of cattle are worshipped.

To quote one authority: 'These examples effectively illustrate that the Taiwanese are quite haphazard in their worship. In their search for prosperity and security, they are willing to worship anything which they think has power to help or harm them. The underlying principle here is that the more gods you worship, the better are your chances of preserving the good life.'

The villagers do not stop there, when it comes to seeking protection from the gods. They are also likely to consult the divine guidance of another set of local gods, called *Da Wang* in Hong Kong (or Great Kings). These are senior in rank to the great-uncles and great-aunts and have shrines of their own, though they are usually very simple shrines: no images or statues, but just a tablet of stone, an altar and probably an inscription or two. These are particularly associated with the big festivals each year, which is when they get their major share of attention and, like the great-uncles and great-aunts, they are thought to be keeping a beneficent eye on events in the village.

A third species of local gods are the Earth Gods and the Household Gods. The Earth Gods, called the *Tu Di*, are the traditional nature spirits which are thought to live in the ground and are associated with the fertility and production of crops, which obviously used to be of paramount importance in all Chinese communities and

still is in the rural ones. Both rural Hong Kong and
Taiwan boast many Earth Gods, as each locality has its
own resident deities. The form of an Earth God may be
very primitive indeed, just a shapeless or worn clay
figure may represent what is, in one way, one of the most
powerful influences on an agricultural community. Even
when an area becomes developed, as has happened in
much of rural Hong Kong, the Earth Gods are usually
still respected and given honour.

The Household Gods form a tripartite union of their
own – the Kitchen Gods, the Door Gods and the Earth
Gods of an individual household. There is one dominant
Kitchen God, Zao Jun Shen, who has his own altar in
almost every household. Despite this, he rates little
attention for most of the year and only comes into his
own at around the Chinese Lunar New Year when he is
supposed to report on the family doings for the year as
mentioned earlier. In some communities, after the New
Year worship his image is burned up and therefore freed
to go to heaven, a new image replacing it once it is
considered that he will have finished the heavenly school
reports. In some villages, the Kitchen God is disappear-
ing, mainly because the kitchen chimney itself is dis-
appearing and that used to be his sitting place.

All of these gods are known as *shen*, a term with a wide
and complex meaning in Chinese society. *Shen* encom-
passes also those spirits which possess mediums – all
kinds of mediums from the *Fu Kay* practitioner to the
women spirit mediums to the healers in the temples.

The term *shen* is used again when the Chinese come to
their theories about the soul. Typically, there is, of
course, no agreement on the structure, role or nature of
the soul. However, there are some generally accepted
theories, which is as precise as we can expect to be. The
human soul has two components – the *hun*, or higher
soul, and the *bor*, or lower soul. The spiritual elements
underlying both *hun* and *bor* are known as *shen* and *gwei*.
The *gwei* are also known as ghosts or demons and it is
they who go around causing all the problems which

plague humans: they make them sick, take possession of them, haunt their houses, bring misfortune down on their families and so on. The reason for this is that, although the human has died, his soul is still held down to its earthly desires and hungers by the strong *gwei* who is unwilling to let go of life on earth. Many of the complex death rituals which the family carry out on behalf of those who have died are to encourage the *gwei* to let go of its hold on the earth and pass on through the underworld to whatever existence is to come.

As to what the life to come may be, there is – of course – no agreement on that either. Chinese Buddhism postulates the existence of a number of hells and a state something like the Christian purgatory through which the soul must work off its karmic debts. Taoism offers a wide variety of beliefs about the afterlife, some of which claim that there is none. Common Chinese opinion inclines towards a sort of afterlife of somewhat vague dimensions, perhaps something very like this life on earth – hence the many material goods which are transferred to the underworld on behalf of the dead – or perhaps suggesting reincarnation. There are many popular tales of reincarnation which people recount to each other. One which was popular in Hong Kong concerns a very rich widow who ferries her pet dog around in a luxurious limousine and at home keeps him on silken cushions to be fed on the most tasty delicacies she can devise for him. Of course, rich women spoiling their dogs is nothing new, but this dog – so goes the story – is the reincarnation of her husband. When her husband died just a few years previously, his widow was inconsolable, certainly beyond the bounds of her wifely duty. Her family and friends became alarmed at the great distress shown by the widow and they urged her to consult a fortune-teller to find out how her husband was faring in the afterlife, in the hope that this might alleviate her grief somewhat.

The widow went to a famous fortune-teller and asked him how her poor husband was getting on in the afterlife.

The fortune-teller went into a trance to try to locate the spirit of the dead man and check on his well-being. Eventually he emerged from his trance.

'Well?' said the woman eagerly. 'How is my husband? Could you find him?'

'Yes,' nodded the fortune-teller, 'and I have some very good news for you. You can be reconciled with him if you wish.'

He then went on to explain that the husband's soul had just been reincarnated. He had returned to the earth, this time as a dog. He described the husband's new guise and told her where she could find him. The widow did not hesitate, but hastened off to the address given her by the fortune-teller. Sure enough, the rather astonished house-holder who opened his door to this somewhat distraught widow confirmed that his bitch had just given birth to a litter of puppies – although how this strange woman could have known of an event scarcely half an hour old, he did not know – and yes, there was one which fitted her description exactly. As soon as she could, the widow took this young pup home and proceeded to treat him to a life of the utmost luxury. Presumably, this somewhat smug dog can still be seen cruising around Hong Kong in his luxury car, paid for by the profits of a previous life.

It is uncertain where stories like this fit into either orthodox or Taoist cosmology – or indeed whether they do at all – but they are typical of the many tales which pass happily round a Chinese community, often emerging in answer to questions which people ask about the origins of their problems in this life. For example, Dan Rocovits tells this story from Taiwan.

A married woman went to see a medium in a temple and told him that life was so bad that she was going to commit suicide. She was married to a man who constantly beat her. No matter what she did, no matter how hard she tried to get his goodwill, he would always end up by beating her and she could bear it no longer. She came to the medium to find out why her life was so wretchedly unhappy.

'My parents didn't choose this man for me,' she explained. 'I myself chose him and therefore it must be that in some way I deserve what's happening, but I don't understand why.

The medium went into a trance and his god spoke through him and told the woman to go home.

'In a few days, a monk will come to your house and ask for money to build a temple. Tell him your problem and he will be able to help you.'

In a few days' time, a monk did come by asking for money to help build a temple. The woman gave him some money and began to explain her troubles to him. He listened patiently and then explained the following to her.

'In your last life,' he said, 'you were a farmer and your husband in this life was a cow during his last life. You owned that cow and, although she worked very hard to give you milk and to help with the ploughing of your land, you were always beating it. Eventually, when that cow died, it went to the underworld and sought retribution from Yen Lo Wang, the god of hell. Because of that, you are being paid back in this life for the misery you inflicted in the last one, and that's why your husband in this life beats you so.'

The woman then asked if she could pay off her debt to him in one fell swoop. The monk told her to go to the market and buy plenty of good food and one straw mat.

'Get rid of everything else in the house that he could possibly use to beat you, roll up the straw mat very tightly and place it in the middle of the living room where he'll see it. Then cook the food and start eating it before he gets home.' This last was sure to provoke a beating since the woman of the house was always supposed to eat after the man.

The husband came home and found his wife already eating. He looked around for something to beat her with and seized hold of the straw mat. As he did so, he became possessed and as he struck her he cried out, 'Paid back! Paid back!' He was frightened by this and asked her what was going on. She told him the whole story and said that each tiny straw in the mat represented a thousand beatings, so that with each stroke he was wiping out her debt from the previous life. Much impressed by this, from that day forth the man no longer beat his wife and the couple today live in comparative harmony.

All this is very low level folklore and there is a much higher aspect to Chinese beliefs, but one which involves ordinary people much less. This is the tradition of the *Hsien*, a word which can be translated as 'immortal', although not all *Hsien* are immortal. The *Hsien*, both immortal and mortal, are the guardians of the inner tradition of Chinese culture, of a hidden path into the secret heart of China which is seldom explored even by the Chinese, let alone by outsiders. The little experience that I have of this tradition comes from a mystic living and meditating today in Hong Kong.

I had been introduced to him by mutual friends who thought that he might be willing to talk to me about the beliefs of those Chinese who are interested in inner development. I began by telling him that I was surprised that there seemed to be very little of the mystical tradition left in Chinese culture and he had smiled at this.

'Many people think that,' he said. 'Even the Chinese think it, but of course they're wrong. There is a very long-founded tradition within China, a path which many people, even in China itself, are following still today.'

I asked him how he knew about it.

'When I was a young man in China, I was very sick indeed. That wasn't very uncommon, you know. There was a lot of suffering in China then. I had malnutrition, beriberi, tuberculosis, malaria and dysentery all at the same time. I should have been dead. I would have been dead, in fact, but someone saved me. He saved me from dying and he set me on the path which I have been following all my life since.

'His teaching was the secret heart of Taoism, an oral teaching which brings men to the highest realization of themselves. It includes meditation, healing, mystical studies and very strict spiritual discipline.'

Such men and women, he explained, have great powers of which he saw many examples in China.

'Once,' he said, 'I saw a man make lightning from his fingertips. On three separate occasions, I saw the dead brought to life again. One of them was my own cousin who had lain dead all through one day. I went up to her body and touched her and her skin was cold to the touch and ghostly white, and her body was stiff. Then in the evening one of the teachers came and brought her to life again.'

Such teachers pick their disciples carefully because, once done, there is a commitment between them. They teach by passing on what they know of the tradition which can never be written, only spoken.

'Although they are very great, they would seem to you to be very ordinary people, unless there was some need of their powers. Then you would know. They never use such powers for display or for money. In fact, they never seek to accumulate wealth. They seek only enough for food and clothing and to provide for their families. Neither do they seek political position or promotion above other people. You could call these teachers *Hsien*.

'*Hsien* have many forms, which is why the word seems to have many meanings. Some *Hsien* seem like ordinary humble people who quietly and devoutly follow the path until one day they may just wander off to the mountains, never to be seen again. Some of them become Immortals, another translation of the word *Hsien*. It isn't uncommon for them to live for seven or eight hundred years. As they continue to follow the path, they may become divine beings or they may return again in human form. Nothing is fixed.'

He explained that true *Hsien* never sell revelations for money. Neither do they give secrets to the world at large.

'The common man takes a very different view of the spiritual from the mystic. Spirits too have different levels of development, just as men do. Some spirits are attached to the planet earth, some to the galaxy and some can go anywhere in the entire universe. Most Chinese, when they talk of spirits, are talking of very low-level spirits. These are earth-bound creatures who have taken their animal natures beyond death. These are the spirits who want worship, sacrifice and even demand marriages. They are attached to power, you see – to the power of being worshipped.'

I asked him how many *Hsien* there were in the world. 'Oh, millions! Yes, yes, millions. Even here in Hong Kong there are many. I myself have two teachers here and there are others I know of. In China itself there are very many followers of the path and now they spread out all over the world. Anyone who wants to can find them. It is only necessary to look.'

4. The festive year

Ancient festivals in every culture were religious in origin and ritualistic in character and they all fulfilled an occult purpose; this is also true of the great Chinese festivals. Most cultures have also, unfortunately, moved away from their old folklore, losing the awareness of its rhythms and purposes, and this is partly true of many of the Chinese festivals. In typical Chinese style, however, they have retained many of the traditions even though they have lost the full understanding of what they were about.

Of the fourteen or so major festivals still surviving in Chinese communities – apart, that is, from the very local festivals for deities or spirits or special events such as the dedication of a temple – very few remain occult. If they retain anything at all of this, it is evident only in their folkloric aspects and they have often become the excuse for a holiday, which the hard-working Chinese certainly need. In some cases, the festivals are deliberately encouraged by government authorities as tourist teasers, such as

Hong Kong International Dragon Boat Day, when the long traditional rowboats known as dragon boats are raced across the Hong Kong seawaters.

However, there are a small number of festivals which are still very powerfully occult, the major ones of which are the Festival of the Hungry Ghosts, the Birthday of Tin Hau and perhaps also the Chinese New Year which is certainly still religiously important. There are many other celebrations which are important to those who observe them, the Buddha's birthday, for example, and in Taiwan the birthday of the Boy God, and so on.

There are also the two festivals most important for visiting the family graves, the springtime festival of Ching Ming and the autumn festival of Chung Yeung, which involve visits to the family grave sites to make offerings, burn joss sticks and generally devote attention and respect to ancestors. These are certainly fairly joyful occasions and not like visiting a graveyard in a western country. The Chinese troop off on a day's picnic and can usually be seen sitting down happily beside or even on Grandmother's grave to eat their food and otherwise pass the day pleasantly. Outsiders sometimes profess to find the Chinese lacking in respect towards the dead because of this, but that only betrays a total lack of understanding of how the Chinese think about their dead. Dead does not mean finished or gone in Chinese culture. It means no longer of this body, but still part of this world and, therefore, still part of the family.

The most popular festival is the Chinese New Year, the celebrations for which once lasted fifteen days, but are now reduced to about three days or, sadly, even less, in most communities. It has become a family get-together time, rather like Christmas has for many westerners, but it is still heavily ritualized. It appears as a feature of the lunar calendar which dominates traditional Chinese life, although the Gregorian calendar is used for all official reckonings these days. The festival falls halfway between the winter solstice and the spring equinox, which makes it feature some time between mid-January and mid-February and it heralds the start of the new year according to the lunar calendar.

Each Chinese year is named after one creature from the Chinese astrological system. In sequence the years are: Rat, Ox, Tiger, Rabbit (or Hare), Dragon, Snake, Horse, Ram (Sheep or Goat), Monkey, Rooster (or Cock), Dog and Pig. The variation of names is merely in translation rather than signifying any essential disagreement in Chinese. This gives a cycle of twelve, but additionally, each year is graded according to the predominant element from the classical Five Elements. So one year might be a Water Horse and so on. This makes a total cycle of some sixty years before any duplication of years occurs. An ancient legend says that the years got their names when the Buddha asked all living creatures to come to him, but only these twelve turned up. To mark their faithfulness, the Buddha named a year after each of them – a pretty tale, but also a pretty unlikely tale.

The days before the Chinese New Year are ones of frantic preparation. In most Chinese communities – although not so much in mainland China where the holiday has been renamed the Spring Festival – a positive orgy of buying precedes the festival. New clothes are a big feature of the celebration so everyone who can afford it buys new outfits. Debts have to be cleared before the New Year begins, the house must be cleaned from top to bottom, as it cannot be swept during the first part of the celebration – in case luck is swept from the door – and special features of the New Year must be accounted for. Peach trees are bought, 'for good luck', say most Chinese today but in fact peach wood featured large in exorcisms in the past and it is undoubtedly meant to keep away evil spirits. The kumquat tree, which carries tiny and fairly uneatable little oranges, must be somewhere in the home. The name of the kumquat in Cantonese makes a pun with the word gold and therefore it symbolizes the coming of money into the household. It is thought most auspicious of all if these flower or bud actually during the festival, rather than before or after, so market gardeners are kept in a frantic state of anxiety in the months immediately before the New Year trying to keep their peach trees and kumquat trees in the correct state of development.

The household gods, and especially the God of the Kitchen, suddenly receive special attention at this time. It is the Kitchen God who will report up to heaven on the escapades of the family throughout the year, so his lips are smeared with honey to ensure that his words about the family will be sweet. While he is away in heaven, his image is turned to face the wall.

Traditional foods are associated with the New Year festival – sweets made of glutinous rice and sesame seeds, candied fruit, melon seeds – many of them now just associated with good luck and the coming of prosperity, but originally probably tantric foods with powers of fertility and regeneration.

Workers get a special bonus for New Year – at least one month's extra salary, sometimes more. This is a survival from the changeover in China in 1911 from the lunar calendar, with its thirteen months of twenty-eight days, to the solar calendar with its twelve months of varying length. The rather simplistic, or indeed, perhaps rather clever, Chinese population was very affronted to find that it was to receive only twelve months of salary instead of thirteen and the extra month's payment at the New Year was officially agreed – a very agreeable arrange-ment, of course.

There are many more traditions associated with the Chinese New Year. In Hong Kong, for example, there are beautiful all-night flower markets to which many thousands of people crowd to buy their flowers, orange trees and peach blossoms for the next day. Children are supposed to stay awake all night because of a belief that their lives will be shortened if they do not greet the New Year as it arrives.

The first day of the festival is for the family only. The whole family gets together and often members may well come back from Britain, the United States or Canada to celebrate with their family back in Hong Kong, Taiwan or Singapore. Thousands of people from Hong Kong go back to mainland China to see their relatives there and queues for the trains to China can extend for miles down the street near Hong Kong's rail terminal. The ancestors are honoured on this day and new red scrolls are inscribed with long life and prosperity signs. Door God posters are stuck up outside the front door to fend off evil spirits and keep the house safe from misfortune throughout the coming year. Knives and scissors are hidden away so the good luck cannot be severed.

The second day is still for family and usually features a banquet-style family feast. The third day is thought of as one in which family members might quarrel with each other – a reasonable supposition after two days of continuous togetherness – and everyone goes out. The streets are absolutely full and friends go to visit each other instead of their own families. The standard greeting to be heard everywhere is *Gung Hay Fat Choy*, rendered into English in many different ways but meaning 'wishing you prosperity'. Many other rituals are also observed at this special time of year.

The major occult festival is the Hungry Ghost Festival, the one which non-Chinese are least aware of but which is actually the most atmospheric, creating an air of menace and mystery throughout the festival. It is a festival of particular importance to Taoists, the Cantonese and Chiu Chow Chinese and is certainly one of Hong Kong's most powerful festivals. The main rituals are held on the fifteenth day of the seventh lunar month, although the festival lasts for a whole month. During this period, the spirits of the dead are allowed out of hell to wander the earth and seek what comfort they can find: wandering spirits with no family to offer them ritual honours, those whose line has died out or who have unfilial descendants who neglect their religious duties. They have become Hungry Ghosts, ill-intentioned, dissatisfied spirits full of vengeance against human beings. To placate them and try to fulfil their needs, human beings make offerings of joss sticks, food and paper gifts at every roadside, crossroads, temple and street corner throughout the festival. In Hong Kong, the large bonfires and small offering fires at the roadsides every night are one of the visible signs that the Hungry Ghost Festival is on.

The Hungry Ghosts are rampaging spirits who belong neither in this world nor the next. They belong nowhere, have no one on earth to put them at rest and can find no way to go on to the next turn of the wheel of reincarnation and karma. Apart from those who have been abandoned by their living families, they are also the spirits of those who died suddenly and violently and cannot relinquish their hold on earth and those who died at sea, whose bodies were never found and conveyed to a resting place where their family could honour them. They are outsiders – the most horrific kind of spirit to the Chinese, to whom being an insider is the most important thing of all. They are often portrayed as having insatiable appetites for food which probably more correctly represents their hunger for acceptance, rest and peace.

The origins of this festival are claimed to stem from the Emperor Wu (Liang Dynasty 502 — 557 AD), but it is undoubtedly a much more ancient festival than that. The Emperor Wu is said to have had a dream in which he was instructed to organize sea and land rites for the dead. Certainly the festival incorporates Confucius' instructions on the matter: 'Devote yourselves to the proper demands of the people, respect the ghosts and spirits, but keep them at a distance – this is wisdom.' Other sources claim that the festival developed with the introduction of Buddhism to China and certainly the concept of Hungry Ghosts is a Buddhist one. Others say that a Taoist legend claims that the gates of hell are opened by Dei Ching Wong, the ruler of the underworld, to allow the dead to wander among the living. They are allowed this privilege in order to renew their ties with their families and to keep the lineage active and loyal to the ancestors.

To keep these wanderers amused and happy during

their furlough from hell, street operas and all kinds of public entertainments are staged in the streets.

The Dragon Boat Festival occurs on the fifth day of the fifth moon each year, which falls in late May or early June. This is undoubtedly an early rain festival but legend attributes its origin to the death by suicide of an official, the incorruptible Chu Yuan, who killed himself by drowning in 288 BC. He is variously said to have killed himself because he lost the king's favour through corrupt court intrigues or because he was so disgusted by the state of the world. The long narrow dragon boats, which race against each other to the beating of a big Chinese gong, are supposed to represent the boats which rushed in vain to save Chu Yuan before he drowned. Anthropologists consider that it is more likely that this was a rain-making ceremony in which the boats represented the war of dragons in heaven, which was supposed to result in rain. It does in fact predate the summer monsoon and often rains on Dragon Boat Day, as it is supposed to. In Hong Kong, this has become a big tourist attraction as it is certainly a noisy and colourful event.

The Tin Hau Festival is the birthday of the Goddess of the Sea, Tin Hau, and it is held in the third lunar month. It is really a festival of the sea people, who come under Tin Hau's special protection and is usually a spectacular one to watch as all the fishing boats from south China and Hong Kong take part in it, sailing with banners, flags and drums beating to the nearest Tin Hau temple in honour of the goddess.

Another major feature of the Chinese calendar is the Mid-Autumn Festival which falls on the fifteenth day of the eighth month, when people go to open heights to gaze upon the autumn moon. Even in rather modernized and debased Hong Kong, where the moon is usually somewhat neglected, this is a festival which people feel is rather precious to them. It is probably not an autumn harvest festival, as people often think, but more probably an old religious ceremony. In Chinese culture, as in other oriental cultures, the moon was spiritually more important than the sun and it dominated the calendar. Of course, anthropologists have argued over the reasons for this for years without drawing any definitive conclusions about it. Anthropologists are not often farmers and it seems obvious that farming, agriculture and animal husbandry are more closely in rhythm with the moon than the sun, as subtle growth periods for crops are more influenced by the waxing and waning of the moon than the crude day/night divisions of the solar calendar. Planting, germination and water supply are connected more with moon influences than sun influences, just as the phases of the moon have more to do with the menstrual cycle and mental cycles too. It is an arrogance of our time that says that the ancients somehow got to know an awful lot about the sun, moon and star movements but were, all the same, not in the least scientific – too many scholars and academics are guilty of this kind of anthropological doublethink.

One festival in Hong Kong which is both a major attraction for visitors and of great local significance is the Cheung Chau Bun Festival – a mediumistic exorcism. The small traditional island of Cheung Chau is largely given over to fishing and farming, but it always had a great reputation as a centre for piracy back in the days when pirates were more common in the South China Seas than they are now. The so-called Bun Festival, which is an English name and not a Cantonese translation, came about because the island was plagued by wandering ghosts and spirits. As these were undoubtedly the slaughtered victims of the pirates, it is only fair that they should have plagued the inhabitants of Cheung Chau. The festival takes roughly a week and starts on the eighth day of the fourth moon. In the days before the grand finale, no one is supposed to eat meat on the island – a great sacrifice for the carnivorous Cantonese – and street operas and dramas are held all over the island. A series of giant bamboo towers are built, about sixty feet high, on which special buns are placed. These are rather hard, sweet flat cakes with good-luck inscriptions on them.

The festival is presided over by Taoist priests and three deities – Shang Shan, a red-faced deity of mountains and earth; Do Dei Gung, a household god, and Dei Ching Wong, the ruler of the underworld. Effigies of these gods are built and Cheung Chau people pay their respects to them. A grand procession marks the third day of the festival – an extremely colourful and noisy event as it winds through the tiny alleys which thread the island on which there is no vehicular traffic. A huge scramble for the buns finishes the day, as good luck is supposed to follow throughout the year for those who get their cake and eat it too!

5. Talking to spirits: the art of the Chinese medium

There can be few other people in the world who are as involved with their dead as the Chinese. Unlike most ethnic groups, which tend to lose many of their folk ways once they come into prolonged contact with the modern world, the Chinese have retained many of their traditional beliefs and practices and brought them into the twentieth-century world of the United States, Canada, Australia and Britain. And that includes many of the traditions of death – among the most important of which is talking to the dead.

Outsiders, and modern Chinese who are somewhat ashamed of folk practices and the beliefs of the ordinary people, talk a great deal about respect for ancestors and say that a family honours its dead and its ancestors as a duty and a courtesy towards those who gave them life and prosperity. It would, however, be truer to say that the family pay attention to their dead partly from respect, but even more because they fear them. Chinese life at one level has always been, and for many still is, a continuing struggle against the powers of the dead. The living see themselves as besieged by the dead – a great army of churning, restless and potentially trouble-making spirits who could – and do – make life unbearable for the living if they fail to keep their dead happy. The living members of society have a continuing obligation to keep the dead supplied with everything they need, or else the dead will be back to get them. Sickness, madness, poverty, failure and misfortune are the gifts of the angry dead to their descendants and that is why the living families pay so much attention to their dead forebears. That does not exclude the possibility that they also love and respect them, but the real spur is fear. As to why the Chinese are so intensely involved with the dead, that is a question for anthropologists to consider. Suffice it to say that many of the practices and beliefs of today's Chinese community probably had their origins very far back indeed in the development of Chinese society, possibly even in the time of the cavemen.

Most of the ceremonies of dying, death and burial are directed towards guiding the spirit of the dead person away from the family and helping to get it happily settled in another world or even on its way to a further incarnation. In looking at these practices and in trying to understand the many beliefs or even just the rather vague ideas about the dead, the outsider is hindered by the fact that many of them seem to be and are quite inconsistent with each other. Perhaps this is not surprising. China is an enormous continent with a very large number of people of different tribes and tongues who have often developed somewhat different ideas. Even in the same community many ideas exist simultaneously which do not logically back each other up. The outsider has merely to accept that this is so. There is no neatly-fitting world structure which others can examine and understand. Beliefs happen, events occur, interpretations arise. Elements of other cultures are added, facets of various religions are incorporated and the final potpourri is an extraordinary mixture which infuriates those who are trying to find a neat, simple and orderly key to the whole when the average Chinese bothers not one whit about it.

So it is when the dead are considered. When Second Aunt dies and is buried with all the proper attentions, she remains Second Aunt for the family thereafter. They will talk of her spirit as Second Aunt, regardless of whether they are Christians, Buddhists, Taoists or whatever. The Chinese, after all, do not even agree on whether or not there is a soul and, if there is, what form or forms it takes. Taoism often avoids this issue altogether. Buddhism is supposed to uphold reincarnation which it sometimes does in Chinese culture and sometimes definitely does not. Some Chinese authorities say that there are two elements to the soul – one, an animal element wherein reside all the baser instincts, while the other is a more spiritual element which goes on to reincarnation. Others say there are three elements to the soul, while yet other sources claim as many as ten. Despite all this, when Second Aunt dies, she still retains her personality as Second Aunt as far as her family are concerned.

As good psychic insurance, the family will get her the best grave site they can afford, make plenty of offerings to her spirit – anything from incense sticks and grains of rice to a whole roast pig – and carry out their ceremonial obligations at the correct festival times. If anything goes wrong in the family soon after her death, they will assume that Second Aunt's spirit is disturbed about something and will call in a medium to investigate.

The other great fear of the average Chinese family, apart from keeping the ancestors happy, is fear of ghosts and spirits. These are not necessarily the spirits of once-living people. They could be the spirits of a place, or trees and rocks, or they could be the earth spirit of a village, or even the spirits of deities. As we have seen, every village community has such deities, and every household and business has its domestic altar with a particular god or goddess as its main spiritual occupant. If troubles start plaguing a household or a community, they will undoubtedly call in a *fung shui* expert or a medium to try to find out what is causing it.

Although many Chinese believe in these things, they do not tend to handle the actual communication with spirits themselves. They feel that this is a job for experts and this is where the medium comes in. The medium is a vital part of the folk religion of many Chinese communities, whether it be in a simple village or right in the middle of Chinatown, San Francisco. Singapore and Hong Kong boast many mediums, though not nearly as many as more rural and traditional Taiwan. Even the overseas communities in the West have their mediums, at least among the first generation of immigrants. After that, the Chinese often learn to be ashamed of their traditions and choose to talk very little about them.

Many different kinds of people become mediums or are forced into mediumship – few of them voluntarily choose their vocation – but they tend to share some characteristics. Whether they are male or female, they usually become aware of their powers quite young. Towards the end of their teens is when most of them start to realize that they have the ability to become mediums, although one middle-aged woman in Hong Kong claimed that she already knew when she was seven or eight years old that she had remarkable powers. It is notable that many mediums find the coming of their power is preceded by either a serious illness or an accident. How this is actually interpreted depends upon the viewpoint of the individual. Some people think they have been spared death, which their accident or illness threatened them with, while others feel that the event was actually sent to them by the spirits in order to, as it were, bring them to heel. Like the religious vocation, the coming of mediumship is by no means always welcomed and the individual may well fight it. It is a somewhat demanding profession, on the whole, which pays little and has rather an odd status within the traditional Chinese society which sets the medium apart. Often the blind become mediums and, although this looks rather as if it was a career choice – rather than being picked out by the spirits, the blind person picks them out – the blind are traditionally associated with being seers and are considered anyway to be somehow involved with the spirit world, whether they are mediums or not.

If a potential medium tries to resist the advances of the spirits and their demands that the medium should be a voice for them, he or she is often afflicted with continuing illnesses until submitting to them. Then the spirits allow the medium to become well and stay that way as long as he continues to work for them. If he tries to give it up, the spirits will continue to punish him. A western-style psychologist may well consider all this to be the sign of a disturbed or neurotic personality, but it may not be helpful to apply western vocabulary to this situation. Mediumship is really the norm for Chinese society and therefore mediums must exist, as they have a function to fulfil on behalf of others who need their services.

Mediums derive their inspiration from quite a wide variety of sources. One medium may consider that one particular deity speaks to him – the hero Monkey, one of the characters in the Chinese classic novel, *Journey to the West* or *Monkey*, seems to be a favourite of mediums throughout Chinese communities in South-East Asia and is usually politely referred to as the Great Sage Equal to Heaven. It may seem strange that a fictional hero can become an actual divinity, rather as if a Spanish medium claimed to be guided by the hero Don Quixote. However, many of the characters of early Chinese writings had long been popular folk heroes anyway and Monkey is undoubtedly drawn from the monkey king, Hanuman, of Hindu epic.

Other mediums may feel that they are inspired by wandering spirits, rather like the spirit guides of western mediumship, while others have more grandiose ideas and feel that it is the Sage Lao Tzu, the writer of the Way of Tao, who comes to them. Usually the spirits of the mediums are drawn from the middle ranks of the spiritual world, not from its higher echelons. Mediums seldom claim to be inspired by the Buddha or by the Goddess of Mercy, Kwan, in their messages. Whether this is natural caution on the part of the medium or whether the more highly developed spiritual beings simply do not get involved in the business of passing on messages to human beings in this way is obviously a matter for debate.

Another common characteristic of the medium is that he or she may have an unfavourable prognosis for a long life. Their horoscopes often reveal early death and it is thought that, in agreeing to become a vehicle for the spirits, they have effected a sort of exchange deal – longer life in return for co-operation. This is often the case with fortune-tellers and diviners too and it is the reason why all mediums and fortune-tellers insist that it is essential for them to lead good lives and work hard at being virtuous. Most Chinese believe that life can be extended by good deeds.

In 1980, the *China Times Weekly Magazine* in Taiwan actually carried out a survey on this matter, examining what happened to fortune-tellers and mediums who sold their powers for money and led lives of little virtue. The article revealed that those who had erred in this way either became crippled, remained poor despite their efforts not to, died prematurely or had no wife or no grandchildren, which is something of a disaster in a traditional Chinese family. It needs children, especially male children, precisely in order to carry out the rites which will keep the dead – that is, the parents, as well as the rest of the ancestors – quiet in their graves.

Mediumship was common throughout the whole of China in the past and especially so in the southern provinces which, of course, include Kwangtung where the Cantonese come from. Recent newspaper reports from China reveal that it is once again becoming common, much to the disgust of the Communist authorities who have tried to stamp out that kind of thing. It is certainly alive and well as an art in Hong Kong, Taiwan, Singapore, Malaysia and in every place where the Chinese have settled in large numbers, including the United States. Some authorities consider Hong Kong and Taiwan to be the last bastion of mediums, but it is more widespread than people have commonly supposed. It is one of the aspects of Chinese society which modern and western-educated young Chinese tend to scoff at and feel ashamed of and they will often deny that these practices still continue. Sometimes this is genuine ignorance on their part and sometimes it is a face-saving device to keep up a good impression in front of westerners who, they feel, will think the Chinese primitive for believing in such things.

Although this chapter deals with the mediums who claim to speak directly with spirits, it is also true that many of the fortune-tellers and diviners are mediums or claim to be so. Even those who use the pseudo-science of physiognomy and palmistry are often gifted with mediumistic abilities, and certainly the fortune-stick readers, the *Fu Kay* (automatic writing) practitioners and the healers are all mediums. From this, it can be assumed that early Chinese society boasted an extraordinarily large number of mediums.

Many of the mediums found outside the confines of temples are women. These women have a number of different names. One which is often used in Hong Kong is *mun mai*, the meaning of which is 'asking for rice'. The name arose from the fact that such women often accepted a handful of rice in payment for their services and also because a pun on the tone also means spirit medium. Another name commonly used as a title by women mediums is *Sam Ku*, which means 'Third Aunt' but also designates those who are in communion with spirits. This is the name which I shall use in this chapter to describe a woman spirit medium.

The mere ability to see spirits does not presume mediumship. Many people, especially women, have the gift of seeing ghosts and spirits but they have no particular ability to communicate with them. This gift is known as having '*yin* eyes'. *Yin*, among its myriad other shades of meaning, is associated with the spirit world, things supernatural and occult. Women, being *yin* themselves, are considered to be more closely in touch with such things, which is why the great majority of mediums are women. Those who do have *yin* eyes, 'eyes of darkness', usually discover the ability when they are very young and it causes them no particular distress. It used to be thought normal enough for some people to be able to see ghosts. Certainly no one else doubted the existence of ghosts and spirits, even if they were not gifted enough actually to see them. The whole structure of the Chinese world of the supernatural was a complex interrelationship of the occult and the everyday.

It would be very difficult for anyone to estimate accurately today just how much belief people have in such things. The first reaction of most young Chinese would be to dismiss all such things as being solely of interest to their grandmothers or possibly their mothers, and it is certainly true that belief in the supernatural is decreasing. However, until they reach an age when they themselves have to take on traditional spiritual duties, it's not possible to gauge what they really think or really would do under similar circumstances to those of their parents.

In the same way, although most *Sam Ku* are middle-aged or elderly women, it should not be assumed that the young do not have such gifts. It may just not yet be their time to use them. Therefore, it is not possible to draw any conclusions about the possible survival of such practices. As just mentioned, there are many mediums in Hong Kong, and not just in remote New Territories villages either. They are tucked away in tight little urban streets in Tsimshatsui and Wanchai, right among the televisions, neon lights and telephones.

One such woman lives within shouting distance of Wanchai Market and, if you saw her picking over the vegetables with frowning concentration, you would think that she was no different from the hundreds of other women around her. You would probably not even look at her once, let alone twice. She is middle-aged, with several prominent gold teeth, and dressed in the usual brightly-coloured trouser suit. Even though she is one of the most widely-known mediums in Hong Kong, there is really nothing which outwardly marks her in any way. Nor does the impression change when she gets home to her tiny flat, with the television blaring in the corner, the radio on in the kitchen, four neighbours playing mah-jong in the bedroom and a cat mewing outside the kitchen window bars. The floor is bare lino, there are family pictures up on the wall and the only slightly unusual feature of the flat is an extraordinarily large and crowded altar dominating one corner of the narrow living room. One other strange addition is a small stockroom entirely given up to the storage of paper goods, such as the possessions burned for sending to the dead in the world of spirits. The altar is presided over by Taoist deities and sages, with large joss sticks burning and offerings of fresh oranges standing before the gods.

This woman, and many others like her, are rather like spiritual telephonists. They will call up the spirits of dead members of the family to find out how they are doing in the underworld and if there is anything they need to keep them happy. She will arrange 'passports' to the underworld for those who are trapped wandering, not knowing who they are and unable to get to the underworld to begin the next stage of their journey through the afterlife. She will also send gifts on behalf of members of the family and arrange ghost marriages. In addition to this already onerous list of duties, she will tell fortunes and remove spells and evil influences from her clients, after diagnosing them. All this is done for very small sums of money. Her door is virtually always open so that people can just drop by and see her, have a chat, check on their fortune, arrange for prayers to be said for someone sick or a specially favoured family member, like a little grandson, get a good-luck charm written out – any of the myriad little favours which are the province of this woman.

Another important function of the medium is the making of a 'passport' for the dead. I was particularly interested in this ceremony when I visited the *Sarn Ku* in Hong Kong. This 'passport' is actually a printed document about the dimensions of a medium-sized poster, and when it has been properly completed and the ritual carried out, it is supposed to give the dead person a free passage to the underworld to start moving through the long process of the afterlife. I gave the medium the name of someone who was dead and she carefully filled in all the necessary details on the passport. The name, previous address when alive, exact birthdate (preferably with the minute and hour of birth as well) and date of death, all these were noted down on the rather impressive document which also had on it a smart red chop or seal mark, which was the visa allowing entry to the underworld. The medium then laid this completed document down before the altar in the corner of the room.

With the document were included numerous other strips of paper. These were prayer incantations, spells and charms of protection against sickness, danger and bad luck. She also added several sets of clothes for the dead person – paper clothes, that is – and large bundles of hell bank notes.

In this kind of mediumship, there is none of the secrecy, silence and darkness we associate with séances in the West. Broad daylight or bright neon strip lighting, with all the sounds of everyday life around – that is the working world of female spirit mediums in Hong Kong. Neighbours drop by to watch and listen, maybe to collect a blessing written on a scrap of lucky red paper, and the medium herself slips easily in and out of trance, breaking off to answer the telephone in the middle of a ceremony. Some might think this a sure sign of being phoney, but in fact it is a strength of the medium that she needs no artificial trappings.

Anyone who wants to contact a female spirit medium need only consult Chinese friends and someone will be mentioned and an introduction easily arranged. It is only through personal introduction that it is possible to meet these women, but on the other hand, such introductions are not hard to come by. The mediums tend to be flattered rather than alarmed by strangers being brought to them and properly presented by those whom they already know.

Women spirit mediums are discreet rather than secretive and they seldom question their ability or how they came by it. For them, the gift is normal and the westerner's 'how?' or 'why?' is puzzling; rightly so, for all that really matters is that the gift exists. The 'why' is not important and may not even be an answerable query. Nevertheless, of course, I did question the *Sam Ku* and asked her when the gift arrived or whether she was born with it.

'Well, I always knew I'd do this – from very young I knew. Even when I was five or six years old, I knew. No one ever taught me what to do – I just go by my own feelings, that's all. All my life I've done it and talked with the spirits. Several times I've tried to stop but the spirits make me go on. I suppose they'll make me continue until I die.'

While she talked, she was preparing a passport to the underworld, and some gifts for the dead man. These included one set of Chinese undergarments, which I suspected would prove something of a surprise to the dead person should he receive them, and an even more startling set of western clothes. These consisted of a rather loud blue-and-white check suit – Chicago gangster style – a gold shirt with little black spots all over it, a pair of patent leather pumps, a homburg and a fan – the latter presumably against the heat of the underworld – all of them paper. A paper phoenix was attached to all this, the phoenix being a creature which dies in ashes and rises to life again and therefore a symbol of rebirth. She then tossed in several handfuls of hell bank notes.

After this, she carefully started laying out the various pieces of paper inscribed with spells and charms, incanting all the time now. She added, for good measure, a wedding bowl to represent marital bliss for me, two paper tigers and one boat to help me sail across the stormy waters of life. At this point the telephone rang and she broke off to discuss arrangements for a ghost marriage the next morning. Finally she put in a big bowl of rice, rice forming part of every magical ceremony throughout the whole of Asia where it provides the staple diet. She lit big joss sticks on the altar, added some more mandala-like designs to keep away evil spirits. These included several *I-Ching* hexagrams, the figure of the God of Fortune, and strips of red and green paper which represented helpers, earthly and spiritual. They are also the colours of life, red for blood and green for the sap of plants. Over this by now growing pile of papers on the floor, she scattered paper cut-outs representing the figures of all the people I might have harmed and who might be wishing me evil as a result. She cancelled all my debts, including those contracted and still owing from my past lives, and threw in a handful of paper bats to bring me good luck and a bunch of red paper helpers to seal the mouths of all ill-wishers. Then she started the final part of the ceremony.

Chanting in a loud voice, she banged two castanet-shaped blocks of wood together at intervals. Holding a three-sided dagger, with two bells on the brass handle, she stabbed all the evil-wishers and beheaded the two paper tigers. There were two large paper figures, one male and one female, and she asked them to release me, which seemed startlingly Freudian. Finally, everything was consumed in one wonderful blaze in a large inciner-ator in the corner, flames leaping perilously up the walls of her kitchen.

'The spirits of the dead are here with us,' she said. 'The dead man is happy with your offerings. He's smiling. And the evil spirit has gone from you.'

She gave me a small charm to place under my pillow, and also gave me a little red envelope with a ten cent coin in it, for good luck.

In Singapore the usual word for a medium is *Dang Gi*

and it can be applied to male or female. It means a young diviner. As in the case of the Hong Kong medium, the gift descends unexpectedly upon the medium and comes and goes as the spirits will. Unlike the women spirit mediums of Hong Kong, most Singaporean mediums are found in the temples. In Taiwan also most mediumship is confined to temples. When a medium is well known, this is a valuable addition to any temple as a good medium attracts many new worshippers and therefore increased income to a temple.

All mediums believe that they must not use their gifts for profit. No genuine mediums ever charge big money for their services, although it is permitted to accept a small payment in a red envelope. This will usually not exceed two or three dollars. One way to spot fraudulent mediums is to find out who is charging money. It is widely believed by mediums that their gifts will disappear, the spirits will become silent and perhaps even harmful if they try to profit in any way. Interestingly, fortune-tellers believe the same, when these gifts are dependent upon mediumship. This does not necessarily apply to astrologers or physiognomists, whose work does not depend upon the goodwill of spirits and who are therefore free to charge enormous amounts of money for their services – and do.

As well as through illness or misfortune, the gift of mediumship can come in other, even more abrupt ways. At one medium temple in Taiwan, the Ow Hsang Temple in Ja Yi township, the medium described his own experience. One day when he was a child he was walking home from school. It had closed early because there were bombing raids over Taiwan, which was then occupied by the Japanese. He came upon the body of a young girl lying dead in a ditch. She had been killed during the bombing of the previous night and, knowing that it was considered bad for a dead body to be exposed to the sky where the gods could see it, he stopped to cover her body with a straw mat, then continued on his way home. During that night he suffered from chills and fever and was struck blind. He knew that the spirit of the child had possessed him and from that night he was a medium, or *Dang Gi*. In the years of mediumship which followed, the spirit of the child often came to him and in the temple where he eventually worked as a medium a 2 ft 6 in high statue of a young girl was kept.

When powers arrive and the medium is first possessed, there are often investigations into the nature of the possessing spirit to make sure that it is a good one. As the spirits which come to mediums are all middle-echelon powers, it is entirely possible that they might be evil or mischievous spirits looking round to find trouble they can cause human beings, of whom they are often jealous. Every medium, therefore, must be sure he is possessed by the right kind of spirit. The wrong kind could refuse to leave the medium's body, rendering him sick or insane, or could even take permanent possession of him. There are plenty of wandering spirits around and they are well aware that they can escape from the world of shadows if they can only find someone to substitute for them.

Incidentally, it is beliefs of this kind which often cause behaviour among the Chinese which seems heartless to those who do not understand their culture. It is commonly believed, even today, that bad or lost spirits, which are equally harmful, wander about looking for a human being whose spirit they can substitute for their own, thereby freeing themselves from hell by delivering the unfortunate human there in their place. It is these bad spirits which often cause accidents and misfortunes that kill people. They are believed to hang about at the scene of such a misfortune, waiting for the dead to let go the human soul or for the dying to complete the process of death. Passers by are often reluctant to come forward and help a seriously injured person in case a vengeful spirit vents its anger at being frustrated by the interfering busybody who stops to give aid. This explains the apparent indifference of the Chinese to suffering on occasions.

There is also the sense that a person's fate cannot really be interfered with, even when there are no evil spirits to cause trouble. If you save a person from death, you will have the responsibility for that person throughout his life and yours. That is one more reason to discourage outside interference.

The medium in Singapore and Taiwan frequently goes through a far more complex process in the practice of his art than does the *Sam Ku* of Hong Kong. Those who consult him will have to bring offerings for the gods, not for the medium, and be patient until the consultation is completed. This is an account of a typical consultation with a spirit medium in Taipei.

The petitioner went with a friend to a very old building in Taipei City, in which the ground floor was a medicine store and the second was a temple. The temple was a very dark building with solid roof beams showing in the ceiling. The two girls signed in the visitors' book and paid a NT$20 fee (about 30p) for which they were given some hell money, a small rice cake wrapped in red paper and some incense sticks. They signed their birth dates on a piece of yellow paper which was placed on the altar before a Buddha. The medium was a man in an adjoining room, sitting beside an altar with the Eight Gods on it, while a queue of people sat waiting to consult him. The girls also waited to see him, watching the queue get smaller. Many of the people there were obviously very sick and wanting to know why they were ill and what they should do about it in occult terms. People often believe that it is evil actions or evil spirits which cause sickness.

One older woman asked the *Dang Gi* why she was sick and he explained that it was because her fate was destined to be unfortunate. He told her to continue seeing her doctor and to take the medicine the doctor prescribed. Eventually the girls' turn came and they spoke to the *Dang Gi*. One of them wanted to ask about a new business venture and the *Dang Gi* asked her whether she had already started the business. No, she said, not yet.

Good, replied the *Dang Gi*, because to have put money into that venture would have been like pouring sand into the sea. 'Wait until you are thirty eight years old before you go into business, then do it and you'll have good fortune.'

Many consultations are like this – particular questions on certain matters, with sickness coming very high in the list. An old woman who came to see the *Dang Gi* produced a child's clothing and asked what she could do to help the child. The *Dang Gi* looked serious at this one and warned the woman that the child would be sick for a long while yet, as she had met with evil spirits – the Five Ghosts. Other evil spirits which commonly cause sickness are the White Tiger, the Black Tiger, the Heavenly Dog and Tai Swei. Encountering any of these can lead to serious illness. The *Dang Gi* wrote a spell on a piece of yellow paper, advised the old woman to burn it and put the ashes in a drink which she was to give to the child. A second piece of yellow paper was to be given to the child to carry at all times. Again, spells of this kind are frequently written out by the mediums as part of their consultations.

This particular *Dang Gi* became a medium in an unusual way. He led an ordinary life when one day a friend of his who ran a temple needed a medium for a particular rite. So he asked the young man to try acting as a medium and, when he agreed, it was found that he was in fact a very gifted one. Many people are capable of becoming possessed by the spirits, but few of them can articulate the wishes of the gods and spirits clearly.

Often, among the mediums of Singapore and Taiwan perhaps more than in Hong Kong, the medium shows clear physical signs of possession, in that his body may shake violently both at the beginning and the end of the period of possession. Sometimes it is necessary for helpers to look after the medium in case he staggers about or even falls during his state of trance. When possession is taking place, according to traditional beliefs about the human being's spirit, it is thought that the *hun* (higher spirit or *yang*) element of the soul has wandered, leaving the *p'o* (lower animal or *yin*) element in the presence of the spirit. The *hun* is quite safe while it is wandering from the body, but the *p'o* is considered to be in some danger from the possibility of permanent possession if the spirit should refuse to leave.

Even if they follow the rules of good behaviour and observe the strict religious preparation necessary for mediumship, it is often said that mediums still die unnaturally young, worn out by dealing with the dangerous world of the spirits. It is entirely possible that evil spirits will come nudging into even the most carefully observed ceremonies. In Singapore it is believed that the presence of a menstruating woman in the temple while the *Dang Gi* is working will attract in the evil spirits which always hang around on the outskirts of temple buildings looking for trouble.

Mediums always take the advice given them by the spirits, knowing that they will be punished if they do not. Tsun Jen, an eighty-year-old medium from Taiwan, is a good example of this. The old man lives in one of the oldest parts of Taipei, in a little tile-roofed house, so old that plants are growing out of the roof between the traditional ceramic tiles. Jen is blind now and started to lose his sight when he was thirty years old. At that time he went to a temple and asked the gods why and he was told that it was a punishment for a past life in which he had been a murderer and arsonist. The gods also added that, if Jen wanted to avoid further punishment in future lives, he had better become a medium, but that he must never accept any money, not even the smallest sum, and must do plenty of good deeds. He followed that advice and, despite the fact that he is now a famous medium, he never accepts money for his services. Those who come to see him bring food and useful gifts and so he manages to live, though he is still a very poor man.

Jen's virtues are widely recognized around Taiwan, however. He is always being invited to live in places infested by ghosts or evil spirits because his goodness drives them away. He even gets invited to stay in hotels, for the same reason. Hotels in the Pei Tou district, known for their association with gangsters and prostitutes, are especially keen to give Jen hospitality, since the wicked activities of their guests leave their room vulnerable to the attentions of ghosts and spirits who love to frequent places tainted with evil. When invited on a visit like this, Jen takes his paraphernalia – statues of gods, blessing papers written by himself – and quite often his little granddaughter for company, and the two of them spend a pleasant month or two on the premises while the ghosts move out.

Families often consult mediums when they are troubled, to find out the real causes of their problems and whether they can do anything to set things to rights and therefore to improve their own fortunes. In this way, mediums often become advisers to the family in the same way that fortune-tellers may. Presumably because Chinese society has always lacked a priestly caste to organize such matters and because Chinese religions do not deal very much in highly personal guidance, but much more in the general duties of an individual in society, it is natural that most people would turn instead to those whom they most closely associate with religious matters. And, whatever outsiders may say about the irreligious character of the Chinese, fortune-tellers, diviners and mediums are actually a part of their religious beliefs.

In this way, a family came to consult the medium Jen after one of their children, an eight-year-old girl, had died. They wanted to know what they could do to ease the child's way through the afterlife and if there was anything she wanted. During the ceremony which followed, Jen – who is blind – saw a young girl running from the door of the temple. He described the clothing of this spirit child and, sure enough, it proved to be the clothes she was buried in. The gods spoke to Jen and said that the child had been too young to die and that she wanted to be reborn. This he told her family. In answer to their pleas, he asked the gods if they knew when the child would be reborn. The family were then told that the girl would be reborn that night at 10 p.m. to a family nearby named Ge. The family went next day to check this out and found it to be true. They did not try to contact either the family or the spirit of the child again. The matter was settled.

Another example of calling in the medium comes from Taiwan. An Oh is a medium working in a temple on Tung Hu Island in Taiwan and he tells of an event in which his father, also a medium, was involved.

'Once, in my father's village, a big tragedy occurred and a number of people died. Of course, everyone wanted to know why their village should have something like this happen, so my father decided to take a trip to the underworld, to find out what was wrong. He selected ten good people to go with him and all of them went to the temple and entered a trance. I remember that while they were in this trance, the rest of us watched them carefully. They looked very frightened and some of them were crying out and screaming with fear. When they all came out of their trance, we asked them what they had seen, but my father wouldn't allow them to tell us. He said it was bad luck to give away the secrets of the world beyond.'

Mediums are often called in to help send offerings to the dead or even to make special arrangements for their comfort. An example of this which outsiders, and even some Chinese, find remarkable is the ghost wedding, sometimes also called the hell marriage – this in reference to the underworld, rather than the state of the relationship. I describe a ghost marriage in detail below.

It started, as ghost marriages often do, with a dream. The dreamer was a middle-aged woman. She had three living children, all of whom were now grown-up and married with young children of their own. She also had one dead son, who had died many years before when he was little more than a babe in arms. It had been a great many years since she had given much thought to him. Of course, she had carried out all the proper rites for him and made offerings at the right times. Naturally, he was written up in the family scroll, but he was really little more than a faded memory of a time of grief and pain for her. Sickly at birth, he had died before he even reached two years old of one of those baby fevers that decimated the infants of the Kwangtung Province in former years.

In spite of all this, she was quite certain that the young man who now appeared to her in her dream was that dead baby, now grown up in the spirit world.

'Mother,' he said, 'I want to marry a girl who is living here in the world of shades with me.'

He gave her the name of the girl and told his mother the address at which her family were still living in Hong Kong. Answering him in the dream, his mother promised that she would do as he asked and arrange a marriage for him so that the ghostly lovers could live together in wedded bliss in the spirit world. When she woke up, she could remember every detail of the dream and she decided to try to find the family of which her dead son had spoken. She could recall their name and even the address which her son had given her, though it meant nothing to her at that moment as she had never heard of the family nor their street before.

She said nothing to her husband when she got up that morning, but just went quietly about her daily business as usual. Once he had left the house, she set off in search of the address of her dream. She found it easily and by making some judicious enquiries of the caretaker of the building she discovered that there was indeed a family of just such a name living there, although he knew nothing of their personal history. More confidently she went up to the family's flat and introduced herself and her strangely appointed mission. Instead of, as might be expected, summoning the police, the family welcomed her and made her sit down and take tea with them. Her story came as no surprise to them, especially as the mother of that family had herself recently been having the same dream. In her dream, however, it was the name of the dead boy which was introduced to her, the boy whom her own long-dead daughter wanted to marry.

Although that story may sound unbelievable, it is one which will be found in every Chinese community. Even today, in Taiwan and Hong Kong such marriages take place with some regularity. It happens in Singapore too, even though Singapore is a less traditional place than the other two. Ghost marriages most frequently occur in this way, a method of establishing a contact which has no logical explanation except the straightforward one that the dead do indeed send messages to their families from the world of spirits. The closest most psychologists have come to explaining this phenomenon is to say that somehow the two families must subconsciously have known of each other's existence – an explanation which does not hold much water with the Chinese. Although the most self-consciously modern Chinese tend to deny that such things happen, it does not take much detective work to establish that such marriages have, in fact, been contracted in their own families at some time during the last twenty years or so.

Apart from such mysterious dream visitations, ghost marriages can also be brought about in less unusual circumstances. This happens when a family wants to marry off a child who has a dead elder sibling. Then it is often done in order to keep the social niceties all in good order, with older children marrying before younger, dead or not. This may occur at the instigation of the family itself or in a more spectacular manner. One report written up in the 1930s by an observer in Hong Kong tells the following tale. A man married and had two children, a boy and a girl. The boy died as a child. The man later remarried after his wife's death and had several children by his second wife. Eventually, his eldest daughter was of marriageable age and the family had a lengthy discussion about who should be her future husband. One of the younger children, her step-brother, suddenly spoke in a voice which older members of the family recognized as the voice of his long-dead step-brother. He objected to the girl marrying until the eldest brother had a wife. He then told them of a suitable girl in the spirit world and, as in the first example, gave the name and address of her living family. When they were contacted it was found that a similar situation had occurred within their family ranks too. This story was related by one of the family members who was present at the dead boy's family council.

Sometimes, the decision to arrange a marriage for the dead is made simply out of social obligations. In these cases, there are no dreams or visions or talk of spirits. The family just approaches the marriage broker in such cases – either a woman spirit medium or a Taoist priest are the usual officiators at these affairs – and asks that a suitable candidate be found for the marriage. Then a child of similar family and status will be found by diligent enquiry and a marriage arranged.

The big question that most outsiders have about ghost marriages is 'why?' Why should the dead be married off by their families? Why should they send messages to the living telling of their hopes of wedded bliss? Why does this go on? After all, while nearly all societies throughout the world have their stories of death and the world beyond, few seem to go to the lengths that the Chinese do and very few indeed arrange marriage ceremonies for the dead. The answer seems to be tied up with the intensity of Chinese involvement with the family and the equally intense involvement with the dead, both these forces coming together as a unity in the question of ghost marriages. Some anthropologists tell us that in most societies beliefs about the afterlife are heavily influenced by the shape and structure of society right here on earth. The living invent, as it were, their after-death life style. If so, then it certainly comes as no surprise that afterlife for the Chinese follows very much the pattern of life on earth. And marriage is a very important part of that, effecting the continuance of the family which survives despite death.

It is worth noting that it is not always the parents of the dead children who have the significant dreams which bring about marriages. There is one story told to me by a prominent woman lawyer involving a dream which she herself once had. About three years ago, she had a very vivid dream in which a strange young man appeared to her.

'I want you to arrange a marriage for me,' he insisted, addressing himself directly to her in the dream.

Somewhat astonished by this rather peremptory demand from a stranger, the lawyer protested.

'Why do you come to me?' she asked. 'Who are you?'

He told her and then added pleadingly, 'My parents don't believe in the world of the spirits and I can't get in touch with them.'

He then gave her the details of the lady, also dwelling in the spirit world, who had caught his affections and also the address of her family who were then living in Hong Kong. The lawyer agreed to intercede for him, especially as he had identified himself as the dead brother of her own fiancé, of whose existence and death she had known nothing. On checking out the information given her, she did indeed find the girl's family and she was able to arrange a marriage for the ghostly couple. She heard no more from the young man thereafter and assumed he had retired to enjoy the fruits of his shadow marriage.

There are some interesting variations on the ghost marriage theme, involving the marriage of a living person with a spirit. This is usually done at the urgent behest of the spirit and not always all that willingly complied with by the living partner, which is understandable. One interesting example of this occurred in Taiwan in 1978. Mr Lee was walking along a street in Taipei, quietly minding his own business, when he came upon a curious little package, made from a red handkerchief, lying in the street. That was his undoing, for he bent down and picked it up. Inside he found a gold engagement ring and while he was looking at this, no doubt thinking that this was his lucky day, a young boy of seventeen came up to him.

'Oh, brother-in-law,' said this polite young stranger, causing Mr Lee to look at him with some astonishment, but not as much as his next request did, 'would you care to marry my older sister, sir?'

Then the young man explained. His sister had died some years previously and had recently appeared to her parents in a dream and told them she wanted to get married. She told them to buy the ring and exactly where to leave it. The man that picked it up, she explained, was her predestined husband – that was to be Mr Lee. Mr Lee was understandably somewhat taken aback by all this, but since the determined young ghost had picked him out as her choice, he felt he was in no position to argue about the matter. Everyone in Chinese society fears the anger of dissatisfied ghosts – that, after all, is really what ancestor worship is all about – so he agreed to submit to the marriage. The young man took Mr Lee home to meet his prospective in-laws and the marriage was arranged and the ceremony held. Apart from the fact that the bride was not visible, it followed much the same pattern as most marriages, the only real difference being that the girl's family paid for everything. On the day of the ceremony, Mr Lee went to the house of his new in-laws and took home with him the altar name-plaque of the young woman which he then placed on his family altar in order to gain the approval of his own ancestors to the marriage. That night, when he retired to his somewhat lonely marriage bed, he tucked the plaque in beside him and this represented the consummation of the marriage between himself and his ghostly wife. From that time on he had the responsibility of paying respects to his wife on all ritual occasions and at the Chinese New Year and in return he became the fully-fledged son-in-law of his new family, invited along on all family occasions.

Even more recently, the *China Daily News* carried a report on July 14 1982. According to this Taiwanese newspaper, a 42-year-old man married his wife's sister who had died twenty years previously at the age of eight. The importunate spirit had visited her mother several times, saying that she wanted to marry her sister's husband. With the consent of the sister, a classical traditional wedding ceremony was held at which the living wife served as a maid of honour. On the night of the marriage ceremony, the man had to sleep alone so that the spirit of the dead woman could come to him and the marriage would be spiritually consummated. From that time onwards, the man had a double duty to his two wives and owed ritual duties to the ghost wife.

Another story comes from a newspaper reporter who told me about a ghostly marital drama which involved his uncle. He was engaged to a young woman who unfortunately died before they were married. Later, after he had married another woman, the first one came visiting him in dreams. She wanted to marry and she pestered him and pleaded with him until he felt pity for her abandoned state and agreed to a marriage ceremony. Despite the expense, and the fact that he was the poorest of his family and burdened with several children, he paid for the marriage ceremony and later, when a new daughter was born to him, named her after his dead fiancée. From that time onwards, his luck turned very much for the better and many people commented that it was certainly because of the compassion he had shown the lonely ghost maiden.

The question may still remain – why ghost marriages? Well, as the above stories indicate, they fulfil several functions. The first and most obvious is that they tidy up the family tree. There are no loose ends left and this can be seen to have many advantages, the chief of which would obviously be the satisfaction of the living family. Often fear seems to be the basis for the institution of ghost marriages. Lonely spirits might well, so the Chinese believe, cause trouble for the living and in several of the above tales it is quite obvious that the spirits were visibly restless. Much of the Chinese devotion to the dead arises from the desire to keep them happy and therefore to keep them from bringing misfortune and misery to the living. The spirits of the dead can easily become vengeful and then everyone is in deep trouble. Tied in with this, there is also the desire to keep the dead supplied with enough worldly and material goods to keep them happy in the world beyond and, if this seems to be somewhat naive, it is just another expression of the afterlife being somewhat like earthly life.

One spirit medium in Hong Kong was astonished by my asking why she arranged marriages for the dead.

'It's the nature of man and woman to be together and it's just the same for spirits,' she said, her brow wrinkling in some surprise. 'Otherwise, they would be lonely.'

It was this same spirit medium who invited me to attend a ghost wedding, an invitation which brought me some perplexity. Should I bring presents, I wondered? And, if so, what was it that one gave a ghost couple?

'No, no, just come,' she said and laughed, showing a valuable nest of gold teeth.

On the day of the ceremony I arrived early in her small crowded flat, tucked away on a sooty balcony in the most urban part of urbanized Hong Kong. Seated quietly, I waited for the couple's families to arrive. They were all elderly and the spirit medium – known as *Sam Ku*, which is a title rather than an actual name — told me that she had deliberately not asked about the age of their children.

'They're very poor, both families, and they can't afford to be too fussy. So I didn't enquire too deeply.'

In many cases, the marriage partner is picked as carefully as a living one would be. The horoscopes must tally, the name characters must be harmonious, the family status must match up. And that is only the beginning. After that must come the detailed arrange- ments of the marriage ceremony itself. The gifts must be discussed, the dowry agreed – it is no easy matter to get everything just right. However, in this case, two poor families were just glad to get partners for their dead children. They had each initiated the start of the marriage by coming to the *Sam Ku* and asking her to find someone for their child. We sat beside the great altar which dominated her room and waited while, outside in the noisy sunshine, the street life went on. Eventually we heard footsteps on the stair and in came two rather old couples. Looking somewhat awkwardly at each other, they waited for the ceremony to begin.

In the centre of the floor was a half lifesize cardboard couple, decorated in festive silver and gold paper. Acting as attendants to them stood ranks of smaller figures which represented the gods and goddesses of hell who had to be invited to the wedding in order to keep them pacified. The *Sam Ku* started the ceremony with much praying before the gods on her altar, the setting up of thick, scented joss sticks, the scattering of paper talismans and good-luck symbols, like paper bats, over the couple and much loud, quick incantation to the gods and the spirits. Eventually after about half an hour of this, the *Sam Ku* took the wedding presents and gave them to the couple. It was quite an extensive range – a double bed, wardrobe, television, stereo set, jewellery, even a thermos flask and mugs. The only slightly odd note was that all were made of paper, as are nearly all offerings to the dead. In rich families, the paper offerings can be lifesized cars and houses and occasionally even real gold objects may be burned for the dead. These are consumed in flames and their essence is considered to have been passed to the spirit world. This again is where the similarity of life after death to the life of this world is seen. The dead are sent all those many possessions which they may never have had on this earth so that their spiritual life may be rich.

The *Sam Ku* added a pile of bank notes, to be used to buy those extra little luxuries that one needs in the world beyond, or even to be used for bribing hell officials – just like life. Then she took the young couple, the attendants, the marriage gifts and all the rest of the paper and burned everything up in a sooty incinerator. The couple were now married.

Their parents left quietly and made their way back

down the stairs, off to have a meal of modest celebration at a café round the corner.

Ghost marriages are to be found at all levels of Chinese society, rich and poor, rural and urban – not frequently, but often enough to remind society that the dead too have their desires and must be placated.

The sending of gifts and even money to the dead is quite commonly done and, although the sender might well be a medium, it is something which anyone can do. A family will often burn paper offerings for a dead relative on the anniversary of his or her death, or on the two great festivals for the dead, the spring Ching Ming Festival and the autumn Chung Yeung Festival. On both these occasions, it is customary for the family to visit their graves and they will often send things to the dead.

As in the ghost marriage this is done by burning paper representations of all those things which the dead person had in life or perhaps wanted but never actually had. Once again, in rare instances, real objects of precious metal might be used, and in addition, hell money is sent which takes various forms. In Hong Kong, there are some rather splendidly printed bank notes, drawable on the Bank of Hell, as well as pieces of gold and silver paper representing precious metal coins. In Taiwan, where printing standards are not so high, there are cruder examples of the same thing.

Although it may seem a bizarre practice, it has many precedents. The Pharaohs of Egypt, for example, were buried with their servants and attendants, plus many of their worldly goods so that in the afterlife they would lack none of those things which made life on this earth so pleasant. The Balinese now make similar kinds of offerings to the spirits. They do not send worldly goods, since they tend to be less materialistic than the Chinese, but they give rice and fruits to the spirits, placing them before the shrine so that the spirits may partake of their essence, and then afterwards the gifts are used by the family. Some people cynically assume that the families are merely making a pretence of offering, but the essence principle is a way of offering common to many cultures.

A form of mediumship which is certainly not special to the Chinese is trance possession during which the entranced medium can perform feats which would normally maim or even kill him, and suffer no ill. Trance possession occurs because a god or spirit enters the body of the medium, leaving him free to demonstrate his remarkable new powers and escape unscathed, or almost unscathed. Performances include walking up ladders of razor-sharp swords, thrusting spikes or nails through the lips or cheeks, eating objects such as razor blades or porcelain bowls broken into pieces and so on. Such festivals occur in all Chinese communities and are usually associated with a local minor deity or spirit. They are probably more frequent in Taiwan which is both more traditional and more rural than either Hong Kong or Singapore, though both these places do have them from time to time.

Dan Rocovits attended a festival of this kind in the Fu An Temple at Luchou in Taiwan. The festival was held to celebrate the birthday of Chih Wang Yeh, one of the Five Yehs of mediumistic fame who are often invoked in cases where healing is needed. Chih Wang Yeh is considered to be the chief of the Five Yehs and the festival organizers promised to have fire-walking and the climbing sword ladders as a ritual demonstration of faith to bring the favour of the deities and thus earn prosperity, driving out any demons which might cause calamities or bring sickness. The devotees are able to survive their ordeals unharmed because they become possessed by the Five Yehs and this is supposed to benefit everyone who attends the festival. The other, perhaps more practical, point of such a festival is that it wins followers for the temple and therefore boosts the temple's income.

The sword ladders are usually made by lashing sharp

swords to the steps of a ladder, so that whoever climbs it must place his weight on the blades. In this case there were twenty such swords, each tagged with a yellow charm, which had been written out by a Taoist priest. The charms were to imbue the ladder with the power of the Five Yehs and keep demons away while the devotees were possessed, so that they could not be taken over and destroyed. Triangular flags attached to each rung represented the might of the Yehs' celestial armies. The ladder was held erect by six guide wires.

The first medium was a man in his mid-thirties, already in a trance as evidenced by the fact that he was frothing at the mouth, a not uncommon occurrence during possession. Dressed in rather exotic half robes, he, in common with the other mediums present, had a somewhat scarred body. All mediums are in the habit of deliberately inflicting cuts and and wounds on themselves while in trance and, although these do bleed, they quickly heal and the men show no sign of pain. They had all prepared for the ordeal by fasting, sexual abstinence and secret religious practices. Before climbing the ladder, they circled round, striking themselves across the shoulders with swords. As the ceremony began, other young men in the crowd began to fall into trances also and as each one showed signs of possession, they were stripped of their shirts and given swords.

Finally the master medium began to ascend the ladder, pausing on each sword to rock the ladder slowly backwards and forwards. At the top of the ladder, he stood and hoisted up all kinds of personal objects which the crowd passed him, since they believe that they will gain protection for their house if they have in it some possession which has received the blessing of contact with the sacred ladder of swords during the ceremonies. Once the medium had obliged the worshippers in this way, he made his way down again, winding his body through the swords and backward and forwards, like a contortionist, finally touching ground again, uncut. The last medium to make the ascent deliberately cut his tongue on the bottom sword and let the blood drip on to yellow spells and charms and the people rushed forward to catch this precious blood, believing that it would give the spells greater occult power.

Rocovits again tells of a fire-walking ceremony in the Hsin Chuang district of Taipei, to mark the birthday of the boy god No-cha. On this occasion, the pre-fire ceremonies were very drawn out and involved a great deal of ritualistic fighting against the fire – probably an occult battle against the demons of fire which could otherwise have caused the devotees to burn themselves on the hot charcoal. Finally, an image of the young god was brought out on a palanquin and the priest passed over the red-hot fire, followed by the palanquin bearers and the young boys attending the ritual. Not one of them had any burns.

In a regular local festival in the Kowloon district of Hong Kong, devoted to the Monkey God also charmingly called the Great Sage Equal to Heaven, celebrants climb ladders of swords and eat their way determinedly through fragments of porcelain bowls with no harm. Many people have seen these rituals being carried out and it is most unlikely, as some have tried to postulate, that the bystanders are all hypnotized into believing that they have seen something they have not. If anyone *is* hypnotized, it is more likely to be the participants in the rituals, rituals which will certainly sound familiar to travellers who have visited other parts of Asia.

6. Magical arts:
spells and exorcisms

In most traditional communities, there is always some-body who can conjure up a little rough magic – put on a curse or two, make up a talisman, drive out a demon – and the Chinese community is no exception. These activities are carried out by a number of different people whose duties quite often overlap. They may be mediums, fortune-tellers, diviners, priests and nuns, mystics and healers. Even the *Fu Kay* (automatic writing) practitioners, who do not usually engage in any other kind of mediumistic activity, can write out a spell or two to keep away evil or sickness.

Such spells are so widely in use that they can be bought, already printed, from traditional Chinese paper shops which sell paper objects to be burned for the dead, as well as incense sticks, calendars and almanacs and other occult paraphernalia. Ordinary people can buy them and sometimes do, but mostly they are bought by those involved in the making of spells. The power of the written word is considered to be very great by the

Chinese, perhaps because writing was for so long the sole property of priests, scholars and monks and the few educated people in that vast country.

At every big or small festival spells are on sale for a very small sum of money. People expect to find occult gewgaws on sale at them and buy readily, especially since such festivals are believed to generate great occult powers and therefore increase the power of the spells. One example of this is the Festival of Tin Hau, the Goddess of the Sea, in Hong Kong. The great place of pilgrimage on that day is a small, dark temple built out on the tip of the Kowloon peninsula to which all the junks for many miles around sail with their banners unfurled and whipping in the wind. The many thousands of boat people who have resettled on the land go by chartered boat and huge ferry to the temple, with their offerings and gifts for the beloved Tin Hau, one of the most favoured figures of the Chinese pantheon. It is believed that the spirit of Tin Hau herself comes to rest in the temple for three days and therefore the many spells on sale are considered very powerful indeed. Anyone can buy them and they are thought to give special protection against death by drowning as well as a whole range of sicknesses.

Writing in 1910 on Chinese beliefs, J.J.M. de Groot comments:

The power attributed in China to spells and charms is really so great that we may call it unlimited. This fact is inseparably connected with the phenomenon . . . that words are not idle sounds, nor characters or pictures merely ink or paint, but that they altogether constitute or produce the reality which they express or represent.

This is largely true today, although it could be a subject of endless and unprofitable argument as to how much the Chinese who use the spells truly believe in them. As an analogy, many people would be unable to say exactly why they follow the superstitious practice of throwing salt over their left shoulder if they accidentally spill it. If they were asked: 'Do you really honestly think you will, say, fall over in the street outside and break your leg if you don't throw the salt?' the answer would undoubtedly be no, but equally undoubtedly they would throw the salt next time. Likewise, the practice of touching wood to avert misfortune. Outsiders would spend a great deal of time without reaching any conclusions if they tried to establish how deep the beliefs behind Chinese folk practices are. We can only say that they exist and that people follow them and this is exactly the case with the use and purchase of spells and talismans. Perhaps it can be regarded merely as a harmless form of psychic insurance.

Certainly the power of spells and magic has long been established as a ritual force in Chinese life. Probably, like so many rituals, it derives from the earliest days of society, the days of animism and nature spirits, but soon became adopted by Taoism; even now a very large part of everyday Taoism is involved with magical practices. That is not the Taoism that readers know from the writings of Lao Tzu: the fine, high-minded, very philosophical musings about the nature of reality and man's own ultimate destiny. Nor is it the Taoism that Chinese scholars are proud of or that foreigners become so attracted to, the way that is and is not. No, this is the rough-and-ready, street level, common Taoism of the ordinary Chinese people, the kind of people of whom the scholars are very often ashamed.

The *Collected Fundamentals of Taoism*, the great Taoist canon printed by imperial order in 1598 AD, states quite clearly in its first chapter that charms and spells are the principal means of controlling the spirits of place and nature, known as *shen*, killing or driving out ghosts and demons, known as *gwei*, and of influencing the powers of heaven and earth. But the spells are used for much more lowly and ordinary purposes as well. They were indeed used to tame the gods of the weather and to bring fertility to the land, to drive back armies and frighten off tigers, as well as to guide the spirits of the dead through the afterworld. In addition, however, they were used to keep out the mosquitoes, to cure headaches, to stop rats chewing at clothes and to keep away burglars, and for a host of other domestic concerns.

Most spells and charms are made for a good purpose. Taoism is very firm on this point; occult powers should be used for good and not for evil, for evil may well be visited back upon its perpetrator and the wrath of demons sent down upon him. Therefore, spells are largely manufactured to make the sick healthy, to keep evil away and to provide protection when it is thought necessary. If there has been a death in the house, for example, there are special spells which can be attached to the house to clean it up again by encouraging the spirits to go away. The most common time for the widespread use of spells and talismans is around Chinese New Year when the family will put up spells on the doorways to encourage the coming of good luck and the keeping away of demons for the year. A visitor to any Chinese community at this time will find such papers, usually written in black ink brushstrokes on red, or lucky, paper.

When particular problems affect a person, he is very likely to go to a temple where a medium is well known for the power of his spells and to ask for the relevant help. The resulting spell, written in black on red or yellow paper, is given to the enquirer who is then told how to use it. He may be instructed to carry it on his person, to put it under his pillow when he sleeps or to ingest it, usually by burning it and then swallowing the ashes with water. This is extremely common in Taiwan and reasonably so in Hong Kong, Singapore and around South-East Asia in general among the Chinese. Incidentally, this kind of practice is not confined to the Chinese. In India, too, occult medicine is quite common, even more so in Nepal.

The spells are traditional, so traditional that they can be found in all versions of the Chinese almanac in a recipe section on spells. Many of the most powerful spell-makers, however, have been taught their craft by others in the occult field, while some simply write down whatever their spirits instruct them to do. The spells are not secret, as are those of the western magical tradition, but their power seems to depend upon the spiritual strength of their author, together with, presumably, the degree of belief of the subject.

There are thousands of testimonies to the effectiveness of spells in Chinese writings, written with the same kind of down-to-earth realism that also marks the exploits of the more mystically-advanced Tibetan lamas. Some of these spells seem rather trivial. There was, for the example, the Taoist mystic of the fourth century BC whose clothes were chewed up by rats. Far from being unconcerned with his material welfare, the mystic cast a spell and summoned all the rats in the neighbourhood to him and then proceeded to give them a firm piece of his mystical mind. He warned all the rats who had not chewed his clothes to go away and stay away if they knew what was good for them, but those who were guilty of molesting his apparel were to remain behind. All the rats but one scampered away, leaving the miscreant rooted to the spot by magic until presumably it learned the error of its rattish ways.

On the other hand, the writings of Ko Hung, the scholar who collected and wrote down the hidden mystical traditions of his day as he knew them in the fourth century AD, wrote of many wonders, including the Taoist Ko Yuen who could cast spells and live without food, control ghosts, sit in fire without being burned and sleep in streams. There is also the eerie tale of the dead walkers of Kiangsi Province, of whom stories are still told now in Hong Kong by those who grew up in the small villages there. There was said to be a particular group of people with the extraordinary ability to make dead bodies get up and walk. This was useful in that all Chinese, when they die, naturally wish to return to their own family grave sites. This is not merely a sentimental wish, as it would be among westerners, but an intensely practical one in a society where the dead must receive offerings and also be happily bedded in their graves, for fear of troubling the living. So, when people died far from home, the walkers of the dead were summoned and apparently induced the dead to walk themselves safely home.

Although I have never met anyone who has seen this, for reasons which will soon become clear, in Hong Kong I did meet a man in his late forties who had been present in a village where such an event was said to have taken place.

'I was just a little boy,' he commented, 'about ten years old, and one day my mother came in and said I mustn't go outside or even look out of the window, no matter what happened. Of course, I was very excited by this and I wanted to know why. She covered all the windows and locked them and then locked the doors and she told me that the dead would be walking through our village very soon and no one could go out while they passed through. Everyone believed that you would die if you looked at the dead walking through. The only one who wouldn't die was the person who had this special power over them. So we sat inside our house and, sure enough, after a while we heard the sound of them coming. Heavy footsteps in a steady rhythm. We kept very quiet in case they would know we were there and the whole village was quiet, just the same. Not even the dogs or chickens made a sound. And we sat still for a long time after they'd gone, afraid to go out. And that was how I learned about the walkers of the dead.'

When the dead were safely delivered home, the walker would be paid handsomely by their families, even more handsomely, no doubt, in case they turned their miraculous powers on the living. Apart from some natural ability, the walkers of the dead did their work through spells. There seem to be few such stories coming out of China now, although other occult practices are certainly reviving; presumably, with modern methods of refrigeration and improved transport, such abilities have become somewhat redundant.

Although most people are reluctant to get involved in bringing evil to others through the casting of spells, nevertheless there is an existing tradition of black magic in Chinese culture and one which is alive and well, even in modern Hong Kong.

Practitioners can be found in most Chinese communities in Asia. In Hong Kong such magic is known as the *Hak Tao*, the Black Path, and followers of the way are called *Da Siu Yan*, or Little People Hitters. The Little People Hitters are mostly old women, usually dressed in the very traditional black clothes of old age, who can be found in certain areas of Hong Kong and Kowloon, where they tend to stick in small groups, or perhaps it should be covens.

When someone has an enemy, such as an annoying boss or a feuding in-law, he can go to the Little People Hitter and hire her to put a curse on his enemy. Such enemies are known as Little People, which means small or inferior people, and the job of the Hitter is to smack back at them with some black magic. A Hitter's equipment is usually a bowl of rice, some incense and a pair of soft black slippers. She first writes out the name of the Little Person concerned on a piece of paper, then she sets fire to it and starts beating out the flames with the slipper, while offering the incense and the rice to the evil spirits, whom she is calling upon to punish the Little Person. These are not major death-dealing curses, which the Hitters would hesitate to use in case the evil came back on themselves, but minor annoyances such as illnesses of the non-fatal kind and accidents causing minor injuries. Such wicked services only cost a Hong Kong dollar or two, or, alternatively, the Hitter can be hired to curse the Little Person for an entire day for about ten dollars.

The effectiveness of this method is, however, somewhat in question. I knew of one person who had been paying a regular fee to the Little People Hitters for several years to get back at her boss, who in fact seemed to be positively thriving on it. Results are not really guaranteed and, moreover, the Hitters are not likely to be bad-mouthed by their customers, for fear that they might produce an extra spell or two to take care of complaints.

To use black magic of the more impressive kind, it is necessary to have the birth date of the victim, correct to the exact hour. Without this it is said to be very difficult to gain complete control over someone else's fate and it is because of this that many Chinese claim not to know their time and date of birth, or are reluctant even to give away the day, let alone the time. There is a long-established fear of such evils befalling the individual foolish enough to give away such information. For this kind of magic, it is not necessary for the victim of the curse to know that he is a victim, as it does not work by auto-suggestion. Spells are cast and people are affected by them and there are plenty of stories which support this contention.

One was told to me by a Chinese lawyer in Hong Kong. She told me of a young woman known to her family who became mysteriously ill and never seemed to be able to get well again, although she saw a number of doctors who could not find anything wrong with her. No matter which medical expert she saw, her health became worse and worse and she was understandably becoming very frightened by her condition. At length, on the advice of friends, she went to see a fortune-teller, which is one way in which many Chinese seek to resolve apparently insoluble situations. The fortune-teller, who was also a medium, went into a trance. Eventually, he turned to her and said something very startling.

'Someone is trying to kill you,' he announced.

'Are you sure?' she gasped, at once horrified by the idea and rather puzzled as she had not been aware of having enemies angry enough to wish her dead.

'Yes,' he said, 'there's no doubt at all. Now you must do exactly as I tell you.'

He gave her detailed instructions about going to a particular place and told her what she would find there. He also warned her to say nothing to her husband. Mystified by his directions, and also not believing him, she nevertheless did as she had been told. She said nothing to her husband, whom she had married only recently after he had divorced his first wife. She went to the place and, as directed, looked under a huge stone. Under it, she found, as he had said she would, a crab which was tied and which had her name and birth date written on its shell. It was slowly starving to death, being quite unable to move or feed. She set the wretched creature free and sent it stumbling on its way. From that day onwards, her health slowly improved.

Later, her husband's first wife confessed that it was she who had paid for the spell to be placed on her young rival, in revenge for losing his affections. And – for the cynical – no, it was not the same fortune-teller who had placed the spell on her who advised the second wife as to her course of action!

Belief in the power of spells is still quite common, even among the most sophisticated Chinese. When the head of one of Hong Kong's richest television stations, Andrew Eu, became seriously ill after returning from Malaysia, it was widely rumoured that he had been cursed. Despite the best medical care, doctors took a very long time to diagnose what should have been a fairly simple case of amoebic dysentery, which is not usually particularly serious, and the Eu family desperately called in a *fung shui* expert to try to exorcise whatever evil was causing the unfortunate Mr Eu's illness. Despite this, he died and to this day most people claim that he died from a spell, not from his diagnosed illness.

Another popular method of casting a death spell is similar to that used in black magic in the western world: the use of a humanoid figure stuck with nails. Fairly crudely carved wooden dolls are used for this and the exact birth date of the victim is written on the doll. After that, the magician will say prayers to the gods and goddesses of hell and then hammer nails into strategic points of the doll to cause sickness or death.

Magical incantatations and spells are also heavily used in cases of possession and exorcism. This could be the possession of the person or the occupation of a house or building by ghosts and spirits. In either case, the people affected would be likely to call in someone who could carry out an exorcism and this could be a *fung shui* expert, a fortune-teller, a medium or a priest, or a Buddhist monk or nun.

The subject of possession is an interesting one because it is an area where different vocabulary may disguise what is really going on. Chinese society has long been a frozen one, subject to very exact rules of behaviour. Children must respect parents, students must respect teachers; there are a great many 'musts' and duties in Chinese society. There is no admission of negative feelings and these tend to be suppressed. Wives never show anger towards husbands who leave them alone every night to go out with their younger, prettier mistresses – a very common aspect of Chinese society – children never express rebellion, even at the most outrageous demands of their parents, and so on. Any psychologist would see this as a recipe for disaster and so it would be were it not for the belief in spirit possession. Whenever situations occur that cannot be fitted into the rigid ideas of established society, they tend to be attributed to possession, which is a convenient way of explaining them and also exonerating the person concerned, as well as continuing to deny that such negative feelings can reasonably exist among ordinary people.

One example of this which occurred recently in Hong Kong was the planned exorcism of a fifteen-year-old girl. When I asked why the girl needed to be exorcised, I was told:

'She's possessed by evil spirits.'

'How do you know she's possessed by evil spirits?'

'Well, she keeps running away from home and going down to the port where she sleeps with sailors.'

Such behaviour would have many descriptions in western society, but being possessed by spirits would not be one of them. A friend told the following story about her older brother who had led a quiet sober life, as far as his family were aware, until that moment when he suddenly became an alcoholic.

'He drank nothing alcoholic normally, then suddenly one day he drank a whole bottle of whisky and then did the same thing every day after that.'

The family realized that he had fallen under the influence of a spell and they called in their family fortune-teller.

'You see,' she explained, 'we knew it wasn't psychological. If his drinking was due to mental problems, it would have happened much more gradually. We knew he wouldn't start literally overnight like that. Usually we Cantonese say that, when there is a sudden complete change of behaviour in a person, then he is bewitched. Often he himself doesn't realize it. He thinks its normal, but his family or his friends know that a spell has been cast on him.'

The fortune-teller turned his mediumistic abilities on the problem. And he discovered what he thought was wrong.

'Your brother is possessed by the spirit of a dead girl. He knew her some time ago and she has now committed suicide and her spirit can't rest and has taken him over. She wants him with her in the world of shades and she won't rest until he's dead too.'

Of course the family were horrified by this and asked him what they should do for the son.

'I tell what I'll do,' he said. 'I'll pray every day and make offerings to the gods for a period of eighty-five days and within that period of time your son will recover and be freed from the spirit of this girl.'

So the great praying began. Every day the fortune-teller prayed and made offerings to the gods and every day the drunken son drank a whole bottle of rather fine whisky. When he got tired of his family nagging him, he moved out of the house and continued drinking. On the eighty-third day, he bumped into his mother in the street.

'Look at you!' she cried in distress. 'Look at your eyes—they're yellow. And your skin – that's yellow too.

You're sick. You're going to kill yourself. What a disgrace.'

Embarrassed by his mother's wailings, the son said:

'Look, mother, I have just one bottle left now. Let me finish that and then it'll be the end of all this.'

And so it was. On day eighty-four.

Sometimes possession happens inadvertently, not through spells or deliberate manipulation but simply because people may have unknowingly brushed up against spirits somewhere. Stories on this subject are legion and come from every Chinese community. This story is from Taiwan. A soldier in the armed forces in Taiwan, called Lin, was swimming in Green Lake in northern Taipei. He was a very strong swimmer, but suddenly felt someone or something tugging very strongly at his legs. He managed to make it to the shore to be told that the lake was considered 'dirty', meaning contaminated by ghosts of people who had drowned there. He was warned never to swim there again.

The Chinese believe that, when a sudden or violent death takes place, the spirit of the dead person is disoriented and goes wandering around, not quite aware that it is dead and looking for its own body back again. If not its own body, then some other body will do. Therefore, the scene of any such death is considered contaminated and people will carry out ceremonies there to try to pacify the restless dead and to persuade them to go onward to their life in the spirit world, rather than trying to re-enter this one by possession. In Hong Kong, whenever a major traffic accident takes place, with resulting deaths, people will make offerings on the site of the accident for several days afterwards and then at regular intervals. Otherwise, they believe, more accidents will be caused by the spirits looking for new bodies to inhabit. For the same reason the Chinese are reluctant to have anything to do with the recently dead or the dying. This is not, as outsiders sometimes think, mere callousness on their part. It stems from fear that the spirit of the dead or dying person will take possession of a living person and steal away his life. If someone has a weak *chi*, or life energy, he could be in especial danger of such an occurrence.

Even in Communist China, beliefs in spirits and spirit possession are still very strong. A friend of mine was a foreign language student in Peking. One day she was leaning idly against a wall waiting for a friend. Another student, a Chinese born and brought up in Peking, came along, turned pale and grabbed her away from the wall.

'Hey, what's going on?' she demanded.

'You must never lean against the wall,' he said urgently. 'You will offend the spirits and they will make you sick.'

It is very common indeed for buildings to be exorcised and this is part of the normal duties of anyone skilled in dealing with occult forces. In China, as in Europe, it was normal in the past for the spirits of any building to be placated by a human sacrifice being offered as the first foundations were laid or even as the doorpost was raised. Rumours in Hong Kong constantly whispered of human sacrifice having marked most of the territory's major developments, whether carried out as a semi-official gesture by the owners of the site or as a brotherly action by the workers; but these stories have remained just that – stories.

A typical exorcism tale comes from Taiwan. A traditional small Taiwanese farmhouse had had family after family living in it, each one leaving after only a short period of occupation, driven out, they said, by the spirits which haunted the place. The last family, however, could not afford to move, so they called in an exorcist. Most Chinese would always prefer to move away from spirits rather than exorcise them. They really want nothing at all to do with the occult forces which they are very afraid of.

The medium came along, bearing with him the tools of his exorcism – a black triangular flag, a sword and seven sticks of incense. He set up an altar in the front of the house, calling on the gods to enter him before he went inside. He offered fruit and incense to the gods. Once the gods had entered him, he went inside the house, followed by a second exorcist. They went from room to room while the first exorcist recited incantations and hung written spells on each room as it was cleaned of spirits. Gradually the spirits were all driven into one small room and then the second exorcist came into action. He had a big ceramic jar with him and he went carefully over the whole room until he found the spot he wanted. There he started digging until he came to a collection of bones which were tangled in the earth beneath the floor. It was those bones which had kept the spirits in the house, the bones of people who had been killed long before.

He dropped the bones into the jar and sealed the top with a written spell on yellow paper, and then the two exorcists took the jar out to sea and dropped it into the depths of the ocean, leaving the family in possession of a now quiet little farmhouse.

Apart from the few black magicians who operate in Chinese society, most magic is used to try to make life a little easier by smoothing out problems and removing disturbing influences or sickness and the magicians, like the mediums and the healers, are among those who help society to keep operating in a safe and productive way.

7. Healing:
mastering the life force

As in western society, there are many ways of healing in Chinese culture, all relating to the way in which the Chinese regard the body. Chinese medicine is essentially holistic and it views the human being as a creature who must be harmoniously balanced in his mind, body and spirit in order to be healthy. Where there is imbalance, there will be sickness. The Chinese therefore regard any form of healing as a means of returning balance to the whole system. They do not separate symptoms into individual units, each requiring a different kind of treatment. Instead, the body-mind-spirit forms a complete unit, which will be subject to disruption if disharmony occurs. The disruption could be physical, mental, environmental or psychic and, although the Chinese recognize the difference between each, they group them together as causes of illness. For example, they believe that those who are sad suffer from lung diseases. Their reasoning is that depressed people do not breathe sufficiently – which is why they sigh a lot – and are not

disposed towards taking exercise. Therefore it follows
that the melancholic is prone to sicknesses affecting the
lungs. But also those who suffer lung diseases tend to
suffer from sadness. In the same class of categories,
sadness can be at least temporarily dispersed by a good
brisk walk which will make the walker breathe more
deeply and will help to counteract melancholy. This
circular reasoning is applied to every condition.

Most people these days have heard about acupuncture
– and its needle-less counterpart, acupressure – and the
ways in which it is used in China in medical practice. Its
use as a form of anaesthetic has often been the subject of
articles in the press and has featured largely in the travel
tales of those who have been to China. Most large cities
in the West now boast a number of acupuncturists and it
is not the mystery it once was, although the way in which
it works is still something of a controversy among
western medical practitioners.

One of the basic principles of Chinese medicine – and
the one which causes most problems for the western
intellect – is that there are a number of energy lines
radiating throughout the human body, called meridians,
and these connect the major organs and act as a circula-
tory system for energy. This is separate from the nervous
system and the blood circulation and, because western
doctors have found trouble in locating and measuring it,
many claim that the theory of acupuncture is nonsense.
This bothers the Chinese not one bit. They, and the
Koreans, the Indians and the Japanese, have all worked
quite happily for the past three thousand years on the
assumption that people can be healed through the use of
the meridian system and they continue to do so.

The theory of the system maintains that it is this
circulation of energy which keeps the body healthy.
Where energy is blocked, sickness arises. By pressing on
strategic points throughout the body, the energy flow
can be made to surge – rather like a dam holding back
water until it builds up and breaks through – and break
through such blockages. Blockages can arise for many

reasons: through emotional causes, trauma or injury, bad physical habits or an upset psyche. Acupuncture is considered to be the more extreme method of treatment, while acupressure – finger pressure on the meridian points – is more gentle and more in harmony with the body. This is not really the place to discuss at great length the pros and cons of acupuncture and the meridian system, but in order to understand any form of healing in Chinese culture, it is necessary to know that the meridians exist, for the Chinese anyway.

The body energy which flows through the meridians is known as *chi* and healing is a way of bringing *chi* up to its full and proper strength. Some people say that *chi* would be measurable if the correct instruments were made to measure it, and in fact researchers are trying to do just this, on the basis that *chi* energy may well be some kind of magnetic force or something very similar.

Setting aside the more conventional Chinese healing methods of acupuncture, herbal medicine and manipulation, all of which have been fully described in many medical books for specialists and laymen, there are two less well-known methods of healing which are nevertheless very traditional. These are both forms of occult healing, one through mediumship and the other through the *chi* energy of the healer. It could be called faith healing, except that it does not require any faith on the part of the recipient, so for convenience I shall call it *chi* healing.

Healing through a medium

Sickness often sends people off to consult mediums, especially when the illness has gone on for a long time and does not seem to be improving at all under medical treatment. It is a long-established belief that lengthy periods of sickness may well be due to the malign influences of evil spirits or even just bad *fung shui* and the Chinese will often go to see a medium just to find out exactly what is causing their illness. This is not such a novel idea, of course. It was common before the industrial revolution in Europe for country folk to look for a source of evil when sickness struck a community or when one person seemed to be prone to recurring bouts of illness and frequent reports of witchcraft bore out these community suspicions. It is a belief which has survived to this day among the Chinese, not quite so much in looking for a human source of the disharmony as for the supernatural source.

Psychologists may find many reasons to account for these beliefs. It is, of course, an easy way to externalize their symptoms and thus to shrug off any personal responsibility. This has some virtue to it when it is considered that the Chinese do not accept the negative as a natural part of community life. Just as anger and undutifulness is externalized by using exorcism to purge the emotions, it may be that a sickness is also externalized when blamed on evil forces. This removes any suggestion that the sick person look within for his own motives in choosing to be sick. It may also be due to the fact that the Chinese certainly never formulated any theories to account for infection or epidemic diseases and had therefore to look elsewhere to rationalize their existence and recurrence. It may also be that, with their absolute emphasis upon harmony as an essential of life, disharmony was also explained as due to external forces.

For whichever of these reasons, many ordinary people turn to the medium for help in illness. Most mediums are prepared to look into such matters. The *Fu Kay* practitioner, for example, spends half his time on writing down cures for ailments. The *fung shui* expert also plays a part here. *Fung shui* professor Leung-chi Lau was consulted by one village in Hong Kong when it became clear that an extraordinary number of the staff at a government clinic were falling prey to sicknesses and having accidents. Professor Lau went along to inspect the offending building where all this was happening.

After carefully checking out the site, he discovered the reason for all the bad *fung shui* which was causing the sickness and accidents. There was a funeral home immediately opposite the clinic – surely, anyway, a most inconsiderate siting – and, worse still, the pointed roof of the funeral home was directing bad *fung shui* straight down into the door of the clinic. Mr Lau took care of things quite simply by affixing a *Bhat Gwa* (hexagonal mirror) over the entrance of the clinic. This carefully reflected back all the bad *fung shui* into the funeral home where, presumably, it had already done its worst anyway!

More commonly than calling in the *fung shui* man, sick people will go to a temple where the medium is already especially well known for his ability to heal. This is not unusual in any Chinese community and there are many stories from Taiwan, Singapore and Hong Kong to illustrate it.

Dan Rocovits reports this story from Taiwan. The grandmother of the Huang family had been suffering badly from aches and pains in her joints for a long time. She had been taking medicine prescribed by the doctor, but it seldom seemed to make any difference. The pains became severe and her whole family was worried about her. Eventually, as a last resort, they decided to take Grandmother Huang to see a medium famed for his healing ability. In Taiwan, the gods most often called upon to heal are known as the Five Yehs and five images of these gods are often brought to the house of the sufferer to effect a cure.

The family made the arrangements and on the appointed day two villagers carried the Eldest Wang Yeh – the greatest of the Five Yehs – in a procession to the house, followed by the medium and the temple custodian who had let the image out for the occasion. The image of Eldest Wang Yeh was carried into the house and placed on the family altar. The medium prayed to the god and asked if he would help Grandmother Huang. He checked the answer by throwing the two bamboo pieces to see if the god agreed — which he did. Finally the medium went into a trance and the Eldest Wang Yeh spoke through him.

'Grandmother Huang will not survive the Chinese New Year if she doesn't have divine protection. She will get this protection if she prays to the local earth god. Each day she must pray to the Jade Emperor.'

At this point, the medium went rigid, his jaws clenched, his eyes closed and his arms and legs began to twitch. He started to jump backwards and forwards on the balls of his feet, from one to the other and his hands beat an involuntary rhythm on the table as the spasms continued. He called for a writing brush with which he began to write feverishly on five sheets of yellow paper. Two of these were charms to be worn by the grandmother, one was to be offered as a sacrifice and the final two were to be burned and swallowed as medicine.

Finally the medium said that the illness was originally caused by five minor demons who could be persuaded to leave her body if she burned hell money for them and left an offering of food outside her house the next day to convince them to go.

Grandmother Huang began to feel better from then onwards and regained considerable mobility in her limbs.

In Taiwan, the most common causes of occult illnesses are said to be meetings with various evil spirits. These are usually the Five Demons, the White Tiger, the Black Tiger, the Heavenly Dog and Tai Swei. It was the Five Demons who had caused Grandmother Huang's illness. Not all illnesses are blamed on these, however. Rocovits witnessed another ceremony in which a very sick woman came to visit the medium to find out the cause of her long illness. The medium told her that it was not due to evil spirits nor to a poor doctor, but because her horoscope was weak. He encouraged her to go home and continue taking her medication and follow her doctor's instructions.

Among the spirit cults of Singapore, the mediums regularly hold sessions to which the troubled or the sick will come seeking a cure. People come with everything from headaches and stomach troubles to tuberculosis and cancer. The medium will often talk quite extensively with the patients while discussing their cases, though he does not actually medically examine them, and will then prescribe for them. Whatever medicine he prescribes – and it may well be something very simple, like advice to abstain from particular foods or to keep warm at night – he will also suggest a proper ritual of observance and may give a spell or charm and exact instructions on how to use it. All such practices include a heavily ritualized aspect of advice and this is undoubtedly what gives the patients faith in the mediums and what, in many cases, may lead to a cure if there is to be one.

Many western doctors, of course, decry faith healing entirely but then, quite often these are patients who would not go to a western doctor anyway; they do not trust them and quite often cannot afford them. The fact is that all sick people have most trust in those who use the vocabulary of their own culture – whether that vocabulary is of germs, harmony, viruses or meridians. Between the differences can be whole worlds of experience but possibly the recovery rate is surprisingly similar – although that is for a statistician to say.

Healing through Chi

The word *chi* often arises in Chinese culture and always has a connotation of energy. Every living being – and possibly every inanimate being too, if we accept that atoms are a manifestation of *chi* energy at work – has *chi* energy, needs it, in fact, for life. When *chi* is exhausted, the human dies. It is *chi* energy which circulates along the body meridians in acupuncture. But this same *chi* can be encouraged to circulate better without the use of acupuncture, not only through meditative martial arts, such as *tai chi*, but also through meditation.

It is worth noting here that acupuncture as a medical art came about in the following way. Originally it was only taught to those who were studying a particularly highly evolved form of meditation. Through the disciplines of this meditation it is possible to activate all the pressure points along the meridian lines with the power of mind alone, rather than through the physical touch. As most people know, yoga works in much the same way. Hatha yoga, or physical yoga, does bodily what Raja yoga, the yoga of the mind, does mentally. It is easier for most people to take the way of the body, and so it is with acupuncture.

Originally it was a secret teaching and many aspects, the non-medical aspects, still are. However, it was recognized that it was not easy for humans to follow the road to enlightenment and that many who started out would not complete it. To enable those who left the meditation orders to make a living in the world and not have to become beggars, they were taught a particular form of acupuncture which they could apply to medical problems and thereby support themselves. This is what most people know as acupuncture. But it is also possible to seek enlightenment through acupuncture, or rather through the activation of some of the pressure points. This is part of a secret teaching, and there are those who follow that teaching in China, Hong Kong, Taiwan and now in America.

All healers, whether they work with the laying on of hands, with herbs, or with acupuncture, use *chi* for healing. Many people are misled by the word *chi* into thinking that it is a uniquely Chinese force, which of course it is not. Unfortunately in other cultures, the awareness of the healing force has often been confused with other things. In Christian culture, it has often been called the power of God which has put many sick people off receiving help. Because western medicine so far does not recognize that which is not measurable by laboratory instruments, officially it does not exist. This makes it necessary for natural healers, who transfer what the Chinese call *chi*, to talk in terms of spiritual power or faith in God. That is not to say that healing has nothing to do with the spirit, but it is a pity that everyone has to use specialized and sometimes repellent jargon about it. The Chinese jargon for healing power is *chi*. *Chi* may well, like *fung shui*, be an amoral force. Although healers often identify themselves with spiritual causes, it may be that healing is a fairly natural phenomenon common to many people. Still, at our present stage of awareness, the Chinese regard *chi* as stronger in certain people and they are often mystics or meditators.

Everyone has *chi*, but some people can either transfer it to others or boost it in others. Those who are aware of *chi* can feel it in all circumstances, those who are not feel it sometimes but may not identify it as such. It is felt as a prickling of the skin, usually accompanied by gooseflesh, which fear, powerful feelings, heavy atmosphere, meditation and medical treatment can all produce. This prickling is the physical manifestation of excessive *chi*.

The ability to heal with *chi* can be the byproduct of intense meditation. Two of the people from whom I felt *chi* energy working on me were both meditators, though from different disciplines. Although meditation obviously increases the production of *chi* energy, presumably from the inner balance which it is supposed to bring about, everyone has it. People with psychic gifts are said to be sensitive to it. They are the people who can visit places where there are said to be spirits and feel their presence. One western woman in Hong Kong reported to me that she was walking in the countryside one day and began to feel the prickling which meant excess *chi*. She soon came upon a clearing in the woods where a lot of people had obviously been to leave offerings – in the form of joss sticks or rice or fruit – also presumably in recognition of whatever it was that produced so much extra *chi* in that particular place.

This same woman, because she possessed an extraordinarily strong amount of *chi* herself, was taken to meet a martial arts' master, who was said to possess great powers. The man was rather shabbily dressed and lived in the open-air basement of a building in a crowded part of Kowloon. As she was unable to speak much Cantonese, they exchanged fairly meaningless pleasantries through an interpreter. Then, signalling to her to wait for a moment, the man went over to a hosepipe from which trickled some water. He took a grimy glass with him and filled it half full. Then, handing it back to her, after making an odd two-fingered pass over the water, he indicated that she should drink it. Somewhat nervously, she did so and felt a jolt of electricity go from the base of her spine right up to her head, a shock which was followed by a feeling of elation which lasted for the whole of the day after the visit.

It is not always good to possess a lot of *chi*, however. Another person was told that the particularly strong *chi* operating through her was 'dead body *chi*', which had apparently come from the bodies of the dead she had laid out during her nursing career. This, incidentally, is why the Chinese want nothing to do with the dead as they are afraid of being invaded by the *chi* of the dead person.

Asked what she thought about this judgement, the woman commented: 'Personally I think that what was emerging was a lot of old angers and resentments.' Which may well be another example of the clash between vocabulary and culture.

While it is true that all acupuncturists use *chi*, there are healers who use it without the physical devices of acupuncture, or even the fingers of acupressure. One healer in Hong Kong uses only his mind to direct the force of *chi* and I have both witnessed this in use and experienced it myself, though I still cannot explain it in other than these words. I witnessed his healing sessions with an American Chinese who had suffered a major car accident in the United States in which literally almost every bone in his body was broken. The accident had taken place some years previously but, not surprisingly, the man still suffered great physical pain and considerable limitation of movement. Doctors had told him that they had done all they could and that he would have to cope with the effects of the accident. Being in spirit at least a vital and energetic man, he found it hard to accept that he would have to lead the life of a semi-invalid for the rest of his years. He was in his mid-fifties when he went to the healer.

The healer became involved reluctantly. Not because he begrudged the man, but because his main work was not in healing and he felt the need to pursue his central discipline of scholarship and meditation. However, his wife had pleaded with the healer to help the injured man. They had healing sessions of about one and a half hours per day every day for a month.

The man wore a light bathrobe and lay down on a bed. The healer made a few passes near him which seemed to put him into a light trance, during which he remained fully conscious and could respond to instructions. The sessions were undirected from the moment he entered the trance. He then began to put himself through an extraordinary series of complex and sometimes violent exercises. He threw himself about, though not in uncontrolled actions, with the agility of an acrobat. For a young boy it would have been a hard task. For a severely injured middle-aged man, it should have been impossible. Throughout this series of movements, he groaned and cried out, apparently because the pain was very intense. At times it was possible to see ripples of movement go steadily through his body, muscle by muscle, one set after another, from the chest to the stomach, down the thigh and from the shin to the end of the foot.

'This is *chi* working through the body's meridians,' the healer whispered.

At times it resembled a man going through a version of *tai chi* and this is basically what was happening. *Tai chi* is based upon a series of movements intended to achieve *hin-yang* balance in the body. After the violent exertions of these sessions, the man was brought back out of his trance, sat up and drank down a mug of tea, grinning away and apparently none the worse for his ordeal. There seemed to be no energy loss at all.

After one month of this, he walked out a whole man again, with no pain and no signs of being crippled. In the two years or so since his session, there has been no setback. For those who think I was perhaps hypnotized too, the sessions are on film.

It is really not correct to call this faith healing. It has nothing to do with faith. It is not really a spiritual form of healing nor even a miraculous one. It is the use of *chi* by someone who has a particularly strong *chi* energy himself and can therefore direct it upon others. The reason that such healings are relatively rare is that people who have such strong *chi* are rare. Although certain people may indeed be born with strong *chi*, others can develop it through very great mental, physical or spiritual discipline.

I asked the healer if he could make me feel the force of his *chi*. First he made me stand up and close my eyes. I was not aware of being put into a trance and yet I think I would have to say I must have been in some kind of light trance. It is hard to explain the feeling but it was a sense of somehow not being quite so firmly in touch with the surface of the world as I had been just a few minutes before. I started to rock gently to and fro in a circular movement. When I tried to check this, I was told to relax and let it happen, which I then did. While this circular movement was continuing, I could feel some rather strange sensations within the region of the abdomen. Difficult to explain because they were unusual, but rather like the light, involuntary tic of a muscle, although I knew it was not actually muscular. The only way I can describe it was that it was a 'foreign' movement, not one which belonged to me.

The medium later explained that the strange sense of tic was the movement of *chi* and a few weeks later, in the course of my researches, I came across this sensation again.

I had visited an acupressurist to talk about *chi* and the meridian system and while we were talking, she noticed I was rubbing the muscles of my shoulders which were tense. She came round behind me and worked on some of the meridian points to ease the tension and I eventually left, feeling a bit more relaxed but with nothing much else to report.

However, I woke up exactly at dawn the next day. I had just had a very vivid dream in which the acupressurist had given me an injection. I woke immediately as the dream ended to find the whole of the inside of my body was vibrating gently. I found this slightly startling to say the least, but it was intriguing rather than frightening and I lay there wondering what was coming next. I could also feel at various points of my body the lightly darting movements which I now recognized as *chi* energy. This continued for some time until gradually I experienced a strong physical sense of total relaxation, a looseness of all the body muscles and a feeling of weightlessness, together with a sense of gentle elation. This continued for two or three days thereafter and, although a psychologist might try to tell me it was all a dream, I know better.

Occult hypnosis

Mr Mesmer might have uncovered the art of hypnosis for the West but the sad truth is that the Chinese were there many centuries before him. Hypnosis is used among the Chinese as part of a general occult training and there are occult hypnotists at work who use their gifts in several ways, including for healing.

One such hypnotist works in Hong Kong, but there are many others. They are not all, alas, as scrupulous as they should be, and they usually do not work within the framework of a temple, so do not have anyone to control their ethical standards. However, it is interesting to know something about the training of an occult hypnotist.

The one I met in Hong Kong and by whose work I was quite intrigued had, in fact, been born in Sarawak and it was there that he began to learn the art of hypnotism some twenty-five years ago. His training was a rigorous and somewhat esoteric one which started with the learning of breathing techniques. This was followed by other exercises intended to build up inner power. Each day, exactly at dawn, the young student, Ming, had to be up and out on the beach, staring into the slowly rising sun, his eyes narrowed against its power. There, as the sun rose, he stood and chanted a prayer for inner power. This exercise was repeated three times a day, at dawn, noon and at sunset. On a clear moonlit night, he had to stare at the moon or on a moonless night at the stars. This went on for periods of thirty-six days. He was also taught the hypnotizing shout.

Whereas in the West hypnotists slowly and soothingly talk their subjects into a trance, the Chinese style is to use a shout.

'This technique is very hard to master,' said Ming. 'If it's not done exactly right, I'll just frighten the subject and it won't do him much good. In fact, if he has a bad heart or poor nerves, it could kill him. Usually I shout three times and it takes a lot of concentration.'

He went on to explain what he saw as the differences between western and Chinese hypnotism.

'Western hypnotists believe in technique alone, but we believe we must develop inner powers, a kind of energy, which enable us to communicate with and affect the minds of others.'

Ming uses his powers for the usual problems people take to hypnotists – lack of confidence, giving up smoking, impotence – but one of his interests is to use it to find clairvoyance.

'Once, when I was back in Sarawak, my brother took some tourists out in his boat. The boat overturned and three people were lost in the river waters. Two of them were found drowned, but the third, a woman, couldn't be found. I put my young nephews – five of them – under hypnosis and asked them to think about where their father was. He was somewhere upriver searching for the body but we didn't know where. Four of them could see nothing but the fifth began to describe to us where the searchers had got to, what they were doing and how. Then I asked him whether he could see a body anywhere.

He said, "Yes, there it is – just where the boat over-turned. The body is caught by a tree trunk under the water and it hasn't moved at all." Well, as soon as it was dawn, we took a speedboat and went upriver about sixty miles to where they were searching. At first, they wouldn't believe me, but then we were able to tell them where they spent the night, what their supper was, who was with who in the boats and so on – then they were impressed and they believed me. We took them to where the body had been seen and, sure enough, the poor woman was there.'

He was at pains to explain that it could be a dangerous matter to experiment with clairvoyance in this way.

'It shouldn't ever be done for fun. You could really harm people and when you tried to remove them from the state of clairvoyance, you might find it would continue and you could destroy their mental health altogether.'

It does happen that Ming gets called in to deal with states more puzzling than clairvoyance. This is one story which happened to him. One day, his bell rang and when he opened it two monks were there, with a young man standing between them. The monks informed him that the young man was possessed by spirits.

'We've tried everything,' they said. 'We've exorcized him and prayed over him, but it doesn't do any good. So we've brought him to you in case you might be able to help him.'

The young man was pale and thin and every now and again seemed to have a painful choking spasm. He could hardly speak but explained his problems in a hoarse whisper.

'I was reading a book one day,' he said huskily, 'and I put the book on a window sill and looked up. I saw a woman in red at the window higher up in the next building and I shouted at her, just out of devilment. Then she leapt out of the window and stabbed my book. From that day on, she has never left me alone. In fact, she's taken possession of me. She's a Fox Fairy.'

This may sound like a typical attack of schizophrenia, but in Chinese culture Fox Fairies are very beautiful female spirits, which are wicked. They are always trying to trick mortals into marrying them, so that they can steal their souls, and this one was no exception. She kept whispering into his ear that he must marry her.

'No,' he would tell her firmly. 'You're a Fox Fairy and I'm a human being and I won't marry you.'

Then she would give his neck a vicious squeeze and this was the cause of his choking spasms. Ming started to hypnotize the young man who suddenly spoke to him very sharply.

'Ming! You'd better be careful. That Fox Fairy says she'll harm you. You'll never get rid of her.'

Ming was starting to feel rather unnerved himself by now, but he armed himself with a crucifix and a rosary and plunged in. It took more than three weeks of struggle but gradually the Fox Fairy's voice grew fainter and fainter in the young man's ear and she entirely stopped squeezing his neck.

'Was that an evil spirit or was he, say, mentally deluded in your opinion?' I asked.

'Well, we cannot say there are no ghosts and spirits in the world, but the subconscious mind can certainly influence our belief in them,' he answered very diplomatically.

8. Reading fate:
Chinese methods of fortune telling

The Chinese are not, of course, alone in their desire to uncover the secrets of destiny and, if possible, to gain one up on fate. Nearly all mankind has, at various times, felt it necessary to find ways of peering into the future before it materializes and most cultures have gradually established acceptable methods of doing so. Quite often these methods seem to have emerged across several cultures and there is some basis of agreement between them. Others seem to belong to a particular culture only and other societies find them bizarre. Whether there really are plans of destiny which can be divined and helped or hindered by human action, whether fate is laid out ready for a baby at his birth, leaving him to totter blindly along the already marked path – these are not issues to be considered here. What is certain is that the Chinese have long believed that the future can be read and that a woman may know her fate and they have several well-established methods for doing this. Such methods are still commonly in use today in all Chinese communities, including the huge community on the Chinese mainland – despite the years of Communism which apparently eradicated such decadent and primitive ideas for a while. The latest reports from China tell of a number of publicized incidents involving witches, fortune-tellers and temple practices.

Undoubtedly, we could spend a long time wondering why the Chinese have had so many methods for telling the future. Perhaps the long and tumultuous history of this vast country led to an inbred sense of unease in the world that could only be settled by knowing what fate was to bring. Perhaps the lack of a priestly caste to intercede with the gods, or even a lack of gods in the sense that westerners understand the deities, whether or not they believe in them, perhaps simply the powerlessness of ordinary people, led them to seek ways to strike back at the indifference of the universe by seeking out its secrets. Perhaps the Chinese have actually perfected a range of adequate and efficient ways of foretelling the future. The answer could be any or all of these, according to the reader's individual viewpoint.

For the purposes of this book, it is sufficient to say that the Chinese have a number of ways in which they seek to know the future, many of which are still in regular practice in all Chinese communities. It is obviously still a very apparent need, so much so that in Singapore, Malaysia, Hong Kong and Taiwan, many of the richer families still retain a family fortune-teller, while nearly all temples have at least one and usually several working for them. In fact, it is the work of these fortune-tellers which brings in the income of the temples, certainly not the donations of the faithful. Sadly enough, most temples would long have been bankrupt if piety was the foundation upon which their finances depended. Not that it is quite fair to dismiss religious faith or piety, since the religion of the Chinese has always been very complicatedly tied in with the seeking of fortune or revelations about the future. That it does not quite always appear that way to outsiders is irrelevant – it is seldom easy for those outside a belief system to draw valid conclusions from superficial observations. The fact that all fortune-tellers of any note operate within the confines of a temple, and indeed are often under its patronage or even contracted to it, indicates a close alliance of a religious nature, if it is accepted that temples are religious institutions. This is also underlined by the additional requirements of fortune-tellers, that they lead moral lives and do not exploit their abilities for financial gain, other than receiving the most nominal payments.

Those who say – and it has been said by those who have lived around them, and still is said, for that matter – that the Chinese are not at all religious but are only interested in fortune-telling misunderstand the nature of fortune-telling. It is not a skill to be learned by scientific method, like astrology, for example, or hand-reading, worked out according to the learned principles which govern it. Fortune-telling is the seeking of guidance from the gods and spirits who, because they are beyond the limits of time and space and matter, know what will come. It is an interaction with the divine, the way in which the gods speak directly to mankind, although they may do it through one particular person. The fall of chance and the telling of the future is the voice of the gods. Therefore, when an ordinary woman asks whether her son will be happily married, she is seeking divine guidance by her questioning. According to the Chinese there is no such thing as chance and nothing that is not known to the highest powers and that is why they are free to ask for answers.

The art of divination is thought to go back to prehistoric times in China and very early written references to it abound. Some sources claim that the first references to what was gradually to evolve into the *I-Ching*, or *Book of Changes*, appeared in 5000 BC, but this was a common date at which to set the founding of several systems of knowledge – the first medical writings are said to date from that time, as is the first version of the *Chinese Almanac* – and it is only legendary. It is true that divination was considered to be an important official function long before the Chou Dynasty (1122 BC). The imperial diviners were accorded great respect and were called in to decide the timing for such things as ritual sacrifices and the start of military expeditions, as well as marriages and funerals. In the year 2255 BC, one official picked his successor by divination.

'Submit the meritorious ministers one by one to the trial of divination, and let the fortunate indications be followed. The tortoise and the grass concurred and the Spirits signified their assent,' says the passage from the *Book of Records*, the historical annals of China.

The tortoise refers to the use of a tortoise shell, without its occupant, for divination, which is still commonly found today. In fact, any tourist who visits the great Wongtaisin Temple complex in Kowloon, Hong Kong, will find fortune-tellers wielding tortoise shells. The grass refers to the use of yarrow stalks, one method of using the *I-Ching*, the ancient book of Chinese divination which became so popular among westerners in the 1960s and still has many devotees.

During the Shang Dynasty (1766 – 1122 BC), the eleventh Shang Emperor wanted to move his capital north of the Yellow River, although neither his own officials nor the people were willing. However, when the tortoise shell indicated that it would be a favourable move, they agreed to go.

The *Book of Records* lists the following officials during the Chou Dynasty who held divinatory posts: the Grand Diviner, the Master of Divination, the Keeper of the Tortoises, the Observers or Interpreters of the Prognostics. Another section of the *Book of Records*, the Great Plan, lays down the whole procedure for decision-making during divinatory rituals. It states that five bodies of opinion are to be weighed in such cases: the Emperor, his officials, the common people, the tortoise and the grass. The tortoise was considered more reliable than the grass.

It is more difficult to find out how these precedents for

divination were set. Most early writings attribute their invention to the Sages, the ancient rulers of China, who perhaps can be considered to have been the earliest priests or *shamans* of primitive Chinese society. Whoever, and indeed whenever, they were, they established a view of man's place in the universe that is still the prevailing one: man is a part of nature and through him heaven and earth connect in their powers. These powers affect his life through the phenomena of nature and it is possible to read the meaning of such phenomena through divination. The stars too, in the heavens, affect man's life, hence astrology. The interpretations of the Sages of all these factors is what makes up the act of divination. The purpose of divination was to set up guidelines for the correct course of action in any given set of circumstances, and this is still the purpose of divination in modern Chinese society. It is not, as the foolishly cynical may try to claim, merely a way to exploit the unwary or the superstitious. The underlying focus in divination was to try to discover what the gods wanted of man.

The earliest references to the divining process describe exactly how this used to be done. For example, the tortoise shell was covered with ink and fired until the ink dried up into cracks and lines, which the diviner then had to interpret. This was done from about 2300 BC until around 300 BC, when the key to interpreting this method was lost. It has never been found to this day and modern fortune-tellers employ the tortoise shell by throwing three coins from it, six times in all, to obtain a reading from the *I-Ching*, the book of hexagrams. It is thought that the tortoise was a creature of particular purity and the ancients professed to see in its form the perfect representation of the heavens and earth meeting.

While the ancient use of the tortoise shell has passed out of memory, many of the other ancient methods of divination are still practised now. Those of major importance are the use of fortune sticks, automatic writing, the tossing of wooden blocks, the throwing of three coins, the reading of names and the use of the

Chinese Almanac. The first four all belong in temples, the reading of names is sometimes practised there and the use of the *Chinese Almanac* is purely a domestic affair. In addition to these methods, the Chinese also commonly use the face and hands for character readings, as well as for the reading of fate. This is usually not done in temples as it is not regarded as divine guidance but rather as a factual reading based upon fixed scientific principles.

Fortune sticks

Consulting the fortune sticks for answers to problems is one of the most popular methods of divination among ordinary Chinese. The visitor who enters any temple at virtually any time of the day is likely to find a worshipper on his knees before the main altar, steadily shaking away at a bunch of bamboo sticks in a round container until one of them falls out. These are the fortune sticks.

Using fortune sticks is a very ancient method of divination which certainly shows no signs of waning in its popularity today. The number of sticks involved in the divination varies according to the kind of temple they are used in. In mainly Buddhist temples – although in Chinese communities even Buddhist temples are far more Chinese than they are Buddhist, and have many animistic and Taoist influences apparent in them – there are usually forty sticks. In temples dedicated to the Goddess of Mercy, Kwan Yin, there are a hundred. Other Taoist temples may have seventy-eight sticks and so on. Whatever the number, the method of using the sticks is the same.

The worshipper asks a question for which he seeks an answer. He must frame the question clearly in his mind and concentrate on it while steadily shaking the container of sticks, sloping it towards the altar so that one stick can gradually work its way out of the bunch and fall to the floor. Each stick has a number on it in Chinese characters and this refers the questioner to a corresponding printed text, usually kept under the watchful eye of a medium attached to the temple. The medium, who is in this case nearly always a man, is necessary because the paper slip in itself does not complete the process. It is entirely possible that six people could get the same number and therefore the same printed text, and yet the final interpretation could be very different indeed. One person's promised good fortune could be another's evil fate. The job of the medium is to relay additional information from the deities or ruling spirits of the temple who choose to speak through him.

The best way to illustrate this is to give an example of a typical printed text. The questioner may shake out a number which results in this message: 'Kwan Tung, the respectable and good, helped to send his two sisters-in-law to meet his brother safely.' When we consider that the questioner may have asked: 'Should I send my son to study in Canada?' then it is obviously essential for some other guidance to be given on how to interpret this somewhat obscure message. That is where the medium comes in.

Almost all the printed texts in the temples which correspond to the numbers of the fortune sticks are full of references to old Chinese legends and stories, as well as being written in very archaic characters and style. They have the kind of obscurity which all the best oracles in the West used to have and are almost like riddles, at least as far as the questioner is concerned.

Questions are usually asked in groups, usually either two, three, five or seven, never just one because one is the number of loneliness and oneness is an outrageous concept for the Chinese in their strictly structured and grouped society. The questioner can ask for answers to his own problems or for answers to other people's quandaries. Certainly among the Cantonese in Hong Kong this is one of the most popular methods of divination. They feel that it is more valid because it depends entirely upon chance – and chance has a very important place in the Chinese mind, being not just a random happening as westerners see it, but a revelation of the divine in ordinary life. There is no way that the stick which emerges has been picked out by the petitioner or influenced by his own wishes in the matter. Furthermore, when the medium gives his own additional interpretation, he does not ask what the questioner wanted to know. He will merely say: 'You should wait for three months before acting, then good fortune will arrive. There is no need to despair, but you have to be patient and that doesn't come easily to you,' or whatever his message may be. The Cantonese like the privacy of the fortune-stick messages.

It is, of course, no easy matter to be a good medium for the messages of the gods and, when they are found, such mediums are treasured by their temples. That is because they can bring a lot of money into the temple. Although each questioner may only leave two or three Hong Kong dollars as a token of thanks, throughout a busy day this can mount up to a considerable sum, added to which each temple has several such mediums working for them.

Visitors to Macau can visit a temple with a particularly good fortune-stick medium, the Shui Fat Temple in the Rua dom Belchior Carneiro. The temple is small and dark inside, like most Chinese temples, and is the usual Cantonese mixture of Taoist-Buddhist shrine. Its only unusual feature is that it boasts a particularly fine reclining Buddha statue which the temple claims is a thousand years old and may well be. It came from China during the early part of this century. The temple is also unusual in that it is where Yuen-chi Yuen works as a medium. He is one of Macau's most respected mediums and has been involved in mediumship for at least twenty-five years. He is under contract to the temple, which is the normal way in which a temple seeks its fortune-tellers. It puts contracts out to tender and carefully picks among the applicants, considering their reputation, experience and ability. The temple is well aware that a fortune-teller with a good reputation will bring his followers with him, as well as drawing in new worshippers.

There are several fortune-tellers in the Shui Fat Temple, but Yuen is easy to spot. He is the one with the queue of people waiting to see him. He is also the one who has his listeners shrieking with laughter as he talks to them, for he is well known too for the wit and humour of his judgements and has bent little old ladies cackling toothlessly as he unfolds the secrets of the fortune sticks for them. He has gold teeth which the older Chinese relish as a visible sign of their prosperity, is gentle in manner and gives the impression of being wise without being worldly. He has short grey hair cut into the brush-stubble style of old working men and sports a white vest and a pair of baggy trousers. He is more than willing to talk about his work.

'I began my training at the age of twelve,' he started. 'I used to help out at a small temple, near where my family lived back in China, and that was where I found that I had the ability to be a medium. I learned concentration, perseverance, patience and – above everything else – faith. I had to learn endurance, like the endurance of the Buddha, and I knew right back then that this would be my life's work – to be a medium and work in a temple.'

He also talked a little about the disciplines of the good medium's life, principles which are constantly emphasized by all those involved with such work.

'The most important thing is that I must be honest and sincere. I can't ask questions of the gods just idly, as a sort of curiosity or to check things out for myself. And I don't try to get money from people either or to use my job to gain special advantages. The gods would never answer me if I did that kind of thing.'

Although Yuen works mostly with fortune sticks, he will also advise people of the need for special ceremonies and prayers if it seems necessary and he also takes part in exorcisms from time to time. However, like most fortune-tellers, he tends to stick to his own specialization.

In Taiwan, a popular method of divination is one which is not unlike the fortune sticks, but is done instead with rolled-up pieces of paper. The method is popularly known as *chow chien* which means 'pick out'. The petitioner first prays and then mentally states his question, after which he picks out a piece of rolled-up paper from a great bowl full of them. He unrolls the paper to read the pictures and characters inscribed on them, in which he finds, hopefully, the answers to his prayers.

Automatic writing

Spirit writing is another variety of superstition with which the Chinese are familiar, and it is popular with the *literati* and gentry, as well as with the uneducated masses. It is frequently practised in private dwelling-houses. There are, however, regular professors of the system, and from morning until night they are visited by persons in every rank and condition seeking to ascertain what the future has in store.

The above passage is an excerpt from J.H.Gray's *China: A History of the Laws, Manners and Customs of the People*, Vol II. It was published in London by Macmillan and Co. in 1878 but it is still largely accurate. Spirit writing has a great deal in common with the seances practised in the West, in which the participants sit around a table on which the letters of the alphabet are laid out in a circle and there is an upturned glass. Everyone puts a finger on the glass and the movement of the glass around the table, picking out messages of greater or lesser coherence and significance, is attributed to spirits, group energy or some other co-operating force. Chinese automatic writing varies in detail but it is obviously a very similar idea.

Spirit writing is still as popular now as it was a hundred years ago, except that these days it is almost entirely confined to temples. On almost every day of the week, the Taoist temples of Hong Kong and Taiwan have sessions of automatic writing, known in Hong Kong as *Fu Kay*, even though purists regard the practice as being somewhat undesirable and smacking of that kind of superstition that the temple authorities do not wish to encourage. Still, as it provides a large part of the income of most popular temples these days, it is seen as financially necessary.

It is quite possible for any stranger to wander into such a session any Sunday at the Ching Chung Koon Temple in the New Territories. He will find himself in a small, airy and quiet room, despite the crowds milling outside through the lavishly expansive grounds of Hong Kong's biggest and wealthiest Taoist temple. It was founded in 1950 outside what was then a mere village, which has now become the new city of Tuen Mun. Since its founding, the temple has become deeply involved with social and welfare work and has its own free medical clinic, as well as maintaining the more traditional aspects of Taoist worship and rituals, one of which is to be found in this pleasant room which is a *Fu Kay* shrine.

Fu Kay is a form of mediumship which is more elaborate than many found among Chinese communities and it started amongst the educated classes, dependant as it is upon the written characters of Chinese, with which no ordinary person would have been acquainted in the old days. It is said to have started as a children's game which was traditionally played on the fifteenth day of the first lunar month, the first and fifteenth days of every lunar month being considered fortunate for many other-worldly affairs and activities. The children would pray to the Purple Goddess and invite her to answer their questions. During the more troubled eras of Chinese history, when any public criticism of the Emperors or those in power was unwise or even dangerous – the Chinese of those times having perfected some remarkably nasty and complex methods of executing offenders – adults took the game over to ask their own more pointed questions. This was undoubtedly also why the art of *Fu Kay* was frequently carried out in the privacy of private houses. Some of it, however, did move into the temples and as a safety measure it was stripped of its political aspects, to keep the temples safe from imperial interference.

Now *Fu Kay* is virtually a required part of every Taoist

temple's services. The dynamic young director of the Ching Chung Koon temple, Timothy Yau, commented that the temple authorities were not particularly happy about their followers' adherence to *Fu Kay*.

'We don't officially encourage it,' he said ruefully. 'But we know that people will only go elsewhere if we don't allow it. The best we can do is to make sure that all the practitioners we have are honest and pious people. It's not unknown for some temples to have rather unscrupulous practitioners, I'm afraid.'

A hundred years ago, J.H.Gray described a *Fu Kay* session which he witnessed in China.

In the room of the professor [of *Fu Kay*] stands a small altar, with offerings of fruit, cakes and wine; above it is an idol of an angel or spirit. The votary kneels before the altar and, having prayed and presented the offerings, calls upon the medium to inform him what the spirit has to reply. The professor proceeds with his client to a small table which stands in the corner of the room, and the surface of which is covered with sand. Here he writes mystic characters with a pencil of peachwood. The pencil is shaped somewhat like a T, the horizontal piece being the handle of it. The end of the upright, however, is hooked. The professor rests the right end of the pencil carefully upon the tip of the forefinger of his right hand, and the left end upon the tip of the forefinger of his left hand. The point is made to rest upon the sanded table. Thus supported, it moves – apparently of its own accord – rapidly over the surface of the table, writing mystic characters understood only by the professor and his assistant. These are translated by the assistant so that the votary may have a perfect knowledge of what the spirit has stated in reply to his questions and prayers.

Compare that event of 113 years ago with my own experiences of watching a *Fu Kay* session in the Ching Chung Koon Temple in 1982.

The practitioner was a middle-aged woman named Miss Mok. Miss Mok had rather a sad history, in that she was engaged to a young man when she herself was just a girl and he subsequently fell sick and died. Such a tragedy, as if it were not bad enough in itself, also tended, in the old days, to destroy a young woman's further chances of marriage. She was regarded as a bringer of misfortune and death. Occasionally, in such cases, the living partner will go ahead with a form of marriage with the spirit of the dead betrothed. However, Miss Mok's decision was to immerse herself in the pursuit of religious knowledge and during these years of intense devotion she came to the study of *Fu Kay*.

'I studied the art of *Fu Kay* in China,' she said. 'In my own village there lived a master of *Fu Kay* and I began to take instruction from him. As we went on, I began to discover that I myself had the ability to do *Fu Kay* and that was how I became involved with it.'

Unlike many practitioners she has resisted taking students of her own, believing that people either have the ability in themselves and will find it, or do not. She regards what happens during her sessions as the man-ifestation of a power working through her, the voice of the gods whom she feels to be speaking via her powers.

When she is ready to start the session, she stands in the small shrine room, dressed in a long Chinese robe. She is a devout and quiet-mannered woman in her fifties with very little about her that would stand out in a crowd, apart perhaps from her unusually hooded eyes. Waiting, serious and absorbed, she looks slightly tired but other-wise impassive. The form which the divination would take was simple. All she had was a box covered with fine sawdust and a pointed T-shaped stick. These days the stick is usually made of willow wood, which is valued for its purity.

The box on which the *Fu Kay* was performed was a free-standing structure on Chippendale-style legs, placed before a simple altar over which the God of Mediums presides. Before him stood offerings of flowers and fruit, with fat joss sticks burning slowly. Otherwise the shrine was bare. Other *Fu Kay* shrines in Hong Kong can sometimes be very ornate indeed with glaring *Ching* primary reds and golds in all-too-vivid splendour. The simplicity of this one was very pleasing and restful to the eye.

When people are ready to come in and ask their questions, they hand pink or yellow slips of paper over to Miss Mok's assistant. These have the querent's name, address and astrological details on them and the question. The pink slips ask answers to general questions, but the yellow ones refer specifically to questions about health, which is one of the principal areas with which *Fu Kay* divination deals. Just like the rules of any good dinner party, there are certain matters which are not allowed to be raised as subjects. There are to be no questions about the nature of the gods or religion, no requests for gambling tips and no petitions for cures for venereal disease. A number of practitioners do not need to have the questions written down as their powers are strong enough to divine the question as well as the answer. Miss Mok, however, only deals with written questions.

The first petitioner arrives. A neatly dressed, bespectacled man in his forties, he hands over his yellow form. He works for a public utility firm in Hong Kong and his job involves a great deal of report writing. In recent months he has been afflicted with a severe trembling in his writing hand which obviously affects his ability to do his work and he is becoming afraid that he might get fired. So, this Sunday afternoon, he has come seeking a cure. Once he has given his request to Miss Mok he kneels before the altar. He kowtows three times, then touches his forehead to the floor nine times and remains in that position while Miss Mok considers his case.

She stands quite still, waiting as if for a message or for guidance, supporting the two ends of the T-stick on the tops of her hands. Beside her stands the young man who usually acts as her scribe with the task of writing down anything Miss Mok tells him to. Usually it is the name of the characters which she will call out.

After a moment or two the stick starts to move in a rapid wavelike rhythm which necessitates Miss Mok hooking her fingers round the stick to keep it from flying off her hands altogether. As the resulting squiggles appear on the surface of the tray, she calls out the characters to the scribe and he writes them down. These characters are written in a very special ancient script which is known to few people these days. Sometimes even Miss Mok does not know the characters which appear and, when this happens, she or her helper will go to the Taoist library in the temple to consult a special *Fu Kay* dictionary there.

The engineer from the utility factory keeps his eyes down, the stick keeps flying and Miss Mok dictates her characters. He is lucky to be getting an answer. It does not always happen and there can be rare days when the spirits are simply not forthcoming. After each wild movement of the stick, Miss Mok smoothes the sawdust flat again, ready for the next part of the message. Eventually it is finished and the man gets his reply. It is a list of herbal medicines he should take, together with instructions for mixing them. He goes away, evidently quite happy with his reply.

This is the usual form of the medical answers which nearly always consist of herbal recipes, usually according to the classical principles of Chinese medicine. Otherwise, the replies to questions tend to take the form of very formal classical Chinese poetry which may be simple or very complex, with clear instructions or very obscure ones. In some cases the questioner needs a lot of help to divine the meaning but in others the answer is all too clear.

Timothy Yau, the director of Ching Chung Koon, told of a friend of his who came to the *Fu Kay* practitioner for guidance back in 1973 when the Hong Kong Stock Exchange was doing a roaring trade and fortunes were being made overnight, even by the humblest labourers who had taken to buying and selling overheated stocks. The questioner worked in one of the colony's top banks and was thinking of going into the stockbroking business, but had some doubts about the wisdom of this. He therefore asked the *Fu Kay* practitioner whether he should take the risk or not. His reply was brutally straightforward.

'You look at the river and admire so many fish swimming there. Maybe you think you'd better make yourself a fishing net. Get back to your own seat!'

So, reluctantly, he stayed in his job in the bank and only weeks later the grossly inflated stock market – with all its worthless shares in tinpot local companies – crashed. Today he is one of the colony's top bankers.

This slightly jeering note in the banker's reply is not unusual in *Fu Kay*. It is this somewhat sardonic quality that backs up the belief of many practitionerse that their answers come direct from the founder of Taoism, Lao Tzu. Others say that the answers come from spirits or some of the other vast pantheon of Chinese gods, goddesses and immortals. Some believers warn that there is a danger to the *Fu Kay* practitioners. While they are doing this work they are in trance, however fully conscious they may appear to be. While the body is entranced passing evil spirits can take possession of the person's spirit, possibly resulting in madness. Miss Mok, however, believes that her devoutness is her protection against such dangers.

'Besides,' she adds, 'it is the god himself who speaks through me.'

Gray, during his travels in China in the 1870s, saw one of the most famous *Fu Kay* practitioners of the day at work.

Of the professors, the most distinguished in our time was one named Yam Ma-asow. His establishment at Canton was visited, not only by persons curious to consult the spirits, but by men wishing, if possible, to free themselves from the vice of opium-smoking. Yam undertook to effect this upon receiving from each opium-smoker a sum of money varying from two to ten taels of silver. Men enfeebled through excess used to resort to him, hoping to regain their strength. I observed that to such patients he gave a liquid which consisted of water in which the ashes of a mystic scroll had been mixed.

Today the art of *Fu Kay* can be found among all Chinese communities overseas and reports trickling out from China suggest that, despite official disapproval, such practices continue there. From Taiwan comes this account of one of the very many small village temples at which it goes on.

A local man, Mr Oh, has a father who was trained in *Fu Kay* when he was younger. He had to go to the temple every night where he donned a long blue Chinese robe and worked with two helpers. They covered a tall square temple altar, the Eight Gods altar, with a quilt, over which they placed white canvas. Then a T-shaped willow stick was brought out and given to Mr Oh's father. The helpers held the other end. The congregation of the temple sang and chanted for a while and then Mr Oh's father started to shake and tremble. That was the first sign of the god entering his body. He started to write with the pointed stick and one helper called out the messages while the other helper wrote them down. The process continued for about three hours and the final results were bound together into a book which was handed round the congregation for the advice and guidance of the community.

Mr Oh mentions that his father's classmate also trained in this way, but was inclined to fall asleep during the long sessions. When he did this the stick rose up and struck him on the head to wake him.

It can been seen from these examples that the procedure varies little, although the surrounding trappings may, as does the alleged source of the messages.

Throwing bamboo blocks

This do-it-yourself method of divination is very commonly found in temples in most Chinese communities. Visitors to Singapore and Hong Kong will certainly see it in practice at almost any time if they go into a temple. It is often used together with the fortune-stick method. For some reason, little old ladies in black clothes seem particularly fond of it in Hong Kong, probably because they can do it on their own without seeking any additional help.

The process is simple and involves the use of two carved pieces of bamboo. Many people claim that these pieces are carved in the shape of the *yin-yang* symbol, but in fact the shape came about because the origin of this quick-question device was a split oyster shell, broken into two halves. Now bamboo is the usual material, or sometimes buffalo horn. The enquirer shapes the question in his mind and then throws the two pieces of bamboo down in front of the temple altar. If both plane surfaces turn up, the answer is *yin* or no. If both convex sides are up, the answer is *yang* or yes. If one is up and one down, this – oddly enough – is the most propitious answer of all. The process continues for three throws and the overall prognosis is taken from the results of all three.

Interestingly enough, in Peking dialect, the official language of the People's Republic of China, the name for these blocks is *kiao*, but a different character *kiao* with the same pronunciation means to teach. The answers which come are considered to be the teachings of the gods coming down to human beings.

Eight-character readings

This method of divining a situation is impossible to explain to non-Chinese readers as it is based upon the use of the name characters and date of birth and is related to the kind of characters used. It is, however, one of the most popular quick reading methods among the Chinese and may well be valued even more, simply because it is impossible for anyone other than the Chinese to use.

Using the tortoise or Wen Wang's method

This is extremely commonly used amongst the Chinese. It can be found practised by a number of fortune-tellers outside the famous Wongtaisin temple complex in

Kowloon district, on the mainland side of Hong Kong. The Wongtaisin temple is Kong Kong's favourite, probably because the great deity Wong is rumoured to grant the wishes of everyone who goes there to petition him, which the laws of probability would suggest was unlikely. Still, it is to Wongtaisin – now somewhat incongruously situated right in the centre of a not very attractive housing estate – that people throng when they need help or comfort or some plain good luck. It is entirely consistent with this that many of Hong Kong's fortune-tellers have done the same. A number of them use the tortoise-shell method of divination.

In Taiwan too, the island's most famous fortune-teller uses this method. It is not a difficult one. The diviner takes a small tortoise shell which in fact is more like a dried-out terrapin shell, and tucks into it three old Chinese coins, of the kind which have holes in the centre and are usually called cash. He throws these six times and finally checks off the resulting hexagram in special reference books. As users of the *I-Ching* will already know, this is very similar to the three-coins' method of consulting the *I-Ching*. There are sixty-four possible computations of reading by the tortoise-shell method.

This method is best applied to single questions rather than to complex readings into the future.

Dissecting written characters

This does not seem to be so common in Hong Kong now, although it is widely used in Taiwan and certainly used to be so in mainland China. The questioner first writes down a Chinese character – anything which comes into his head. Then the fortune-teller goes on to dissect the character and tell him what it all means. This can give rise to a considerable reading because all Chinese characters, unlike the Roman alphabet, have many elements of other words in them. It is this multiplicity of concepts in each character that makes Chinese poetry so difficult to translate and explains why two translations may have so little in common that the reader might be excused for wondering if it could possibly have been the same poem in the first place. Obviously a written language so rich in elements is ready made for the fortune-teller's rhetoric.

This is quite an old method of divining and it is mentioned in the *History of the State of Lu*, dating from 722 BC. There are several references to divining according to characters from then onwards. In the Tang Dynasty there was a Taoist priest, Tsui wu-yih, who was famous for his ability in this particular art. One warlord came to see him to consult as to whether it was time for him to launch a crushing campaign against his rebel enemies. Tsui asked him to write some characters in the dust and, from the results of changing around those characters by removing certain strokes of one and transferring them to another, he managed to make a new phrase altogether which was 'Butt him with your horns', which the warlord then did – and won.

Of course, the dubious would argue that anyone could make any word mean anything they chose by turning the characters all around, and by making use of the many homophones in the Chinese language, and this is a fair argument. In the same way, the so-called free-association method of saying words at random which some psychologists and analysts like to use with their patients could equally well be the subject of protest. Most Chinese would simply place much more credence upon the word of a known fortune-teller than they would on a psychologist, who seems as strange and foreign to their culture as the average analyst would to the Chinese culture and its concepts.

Although most Chinese now give very little thought to their preparations for a reading from a fortune-teller, there is said to be a correct way of preparing oneself for such a session, even if it is self-conducted. Ideally, such consultations should take place at four in the morning. They seldom do, but a much sought-after fortune-teller will see his special clients as early in the day as possible. Four in the morning is considered to be the time at which spiritual powers are at their greatest, though they are also strong at dusk. Body and spirit energy, *chi*, is flowing particularly well at this time, with a resurgence after the low *chi* of the night. In contrast, the mortally sick often die around three in the morning, before *chi* has renewed and when it is at its lowest. This is why most religious orders, whether Christian, Buddhist or Hindu, start their first devotions at this time.

The one who wishes to consult the gods should bathe first and should give up eating meat for three days before – among the carnivorous Cantonese of Hong Kong, this would be almost unheard of – and the reading should take place out of doors, free from the dangers of bad *fung shui* which may pollute the session. It should be preceded by an offering to the deities.

Physiognomy and palmistry

Palmistry is considered, by those who believe in such possibilities, to be very significant in outlining the events of life in the West and in many parts of Asia. Among the Chinese, however, hand-reading comes a very poor second to physiognomy. The Chinese consider that it is the face which gives everything away. Only after the features of the face have been carefully examined do the Chinese turn to the inspection of the lines of the hand. They claim that the reason for this is that the face is inherited and its features set from birth, whereas the lines of the hand are very changeable.

Face-reading is a prominent part of modern fortune-telling among Chinese communities, but it is not thought of as having anything to do with divination. It is a fixed science in which the facts and their significance are always interpreted in the same way and it has nothing to do with messages from the deities or spirits. It is therefore seldom found in temples and seldom patronized by them, although it is quite common to find physiognomists nearby as the ordinary Chinese do not see a great deal of difference between the various supernatural consultants they call upon. Any standard, acceptable means of consultation is fair and all will do in a storm when guidance is needed. It is often true that good face and hand-readers are also somewhat psychic and may add observations of their own to straight palmistry and physiognomy.

In Chinese terms, the art of physiognomy is a comparatively recent one to which there are no written references before the Chou Dynasty (1122 BC). Perhaps because of its newer arrival on the fortune-telling scene, historical commentators were fairly hard upon the upstart art. Also, its purely secular origins, based merely upon an alleged system of measuring the features and the observations to be drawn from them, probably also mitigated against it. To most early commentators, physiognomy completely lacked the divine endorsement that they felt most other methods of divination had. It was merely a system devised by other human beings who were obviously liable to make mistakes in judgement, especially as they were only semi-educated in many cases. This would undoubtedly have influenced the fully educated scholars and officials very much against these practitioners of the art.

One commentator wrote somewhat scathingly in the Chou Dynasty: 'Physiognomy consists of minute inspection of the structure of the bones, in order to deduce therefrom whether a person's future will be lucky or unlucky and whether he will be rich or poor. Vain practices which impose on the ignorant.'

A testy refutation of physiognomy was written by the philosopher Sun Tze, whom we know better these days for the much-translated book on Chinese war strategy, *The Art of Warfare*. Sun Tze wrote in about the year 282 BC and said:

Formerly there were no physiognomists and the word is not found in any books . . . It would be much better to speak of the heart rather than examine the countenance, better still to discourse on men's intentions rather than on the heart . . .

A man's exterior, be he of high or low stature, gaunt or stout, gifted with fine features or ugly as a toad, exerts utterly no influence upon his good or evil fortune. The Ancients never noticed such twaddle, and writers did not even mention it in their books.

He then proceeded to list a number of men who were apparently entirely unaffected by their respective physical appearances. Among them was the famous aristocrat Duke Chow, who was rather short, and the learned Sage Confucius whose head had a somewhat squashed appearance. One noble minister 'resembled a fish standing up', while the Emperors Kieh and Chou were well-built, of commanding stature but monsters of cruelty who behaved like tyrants.

'It is not, therefore, the countenance which injures a man,' he concluded, 'but the lack of prudence and intelligence which causes his misfortune.'

However, despite these wise and moderate words, the views of Sun Tze and others like him did not win the day. The art of physiognomy gained increasing popularity and even became enshrined as a semi-officially recognized practice. Today it has become totally intermingled with the other inevitabilities of Chinese culture and thus the features represent the Five Elements, the balance of *yin* and *yang* and so on, as well as having an astrological significance.

Those who are practitioners of the art genuinely believe in their perceptions. This is what one of Hong Kong's most famous physiognomists, Lai-chuen Yip, has to say about his work.

When we consider the face, the most important part is the eyes. That is where the changes in the heart can be seen. There are forty-eight different kinds of expressions in the eyes alone. And ten types of face shapes, each with its character delineation. We believe that there are certain physical attributes which a person should have, but these are different in men and women. Women should have a small broad forehead, but a man should have a tall broad forehead which shows he is intelligent. The pupils of the eyes should be clear and white. The size of the earlobe shows the possibilities of wealth – small lobes show someone who will remain poor while large earlobes show someone who can become rich. A good straight nose shows a good marriage. And so on.

Most physiognomists work from two or three classical guides written by earlier practitioners. The most famous is the *Ma Yee Shang Fa, Easy Guide to Physiognomy*, a Sung Dynasty classic written down by the student of a noted practitioner, who carefully recorded the work and theories of his master. It is this book which is still most commonly used in Hong Kong, Singapore and Taiwan, and the classic is still in print and published by different publishers in each place. A similar work is the *Lau Jong*, which was written during the Ching Dynasty. A third standard text for face-readers is a work dating from the reign of the Emperor Kiang Hsi and called *The Manual of Fortune Telling*.

For all the scepticism of scholars, a man's face did become his fortune during later imperial times. Even though Confucius himself wrote scornfully: 'If we should judge people by outward appearances, we should have lost Tze Yu,' such views fell beneath the gradual onslaught of the belief. The unfortunate Tze Yu to whom Confucius referred was one of the disciples of the Sage. His outward appearance was of unspeakable ugliness, but he had a very fine mind and became a follower of Confucius before eventually going off to the south where he founded a school of 300 disciples. However, it came about that a man could eventually go far by having the right kind of face. During the Ching Dynasty, a man who had failed the Third Degree imperial examinations which decided whether or not candidates could enter official life and the Mandarin class might still be allowed entrance if he had a suitable face. Every three years, imperial selection boards met to consider the cases of those scholars who had failed for the third time to pass into the Third Degree from the Second.

A man with favourable features could still be allowed such an appointment if he had a face of auspicious shape: broad and oblong, broad and square, narrow and oblong or small and oblong. Such features could qualify their lucky possessor for a post as a district magistrate. Scholars with less suitable features were usually advised to take up teaching for a living.

The Hong Kong face-reader, Lai-chuen Yip, entered his profession in much the same way as most of the divinatory fortune-tellers, even though physiognomy is not connected with divining.

Yip is in his sixties now and has a luminously pleasant face which easily lights with a smile. He is the kind of man most people would feel they could trust.

'My father was the one who was interested in all this kind of knowledge. He didn't like studying on the whole, but he did like to read books about fortune-telling. When he was very young, he found a whole batch of such books in his home town back in Kwangtung Province, so that was the start of it all. He was interested in character too. He used to tell me that you could even spot the differences in character between fighting crickets, let alone human beings.'

Then he mentioned an odd fact which constantly recurs among those who are involved with fortune-telling and divination.

'I knew when I was a very young man that I would die when I was twenty-four. I just knew it without any doubt. Everybody told me I was stupid to talk like that and even my father agreed with them. But I really believed it. It was because of that I didn't marry when I normally should have done. Instead I went travelling around China and I met all kinds of people. I often stayed in temples and I met monks, very special people some of them were too. While we travelled together, they told me about the mysteries of the world and the true relationship of earth and heaven. I went on travelling because I wanted to see as much as I could of the world before I died at twenty-four.'

One dark, rainy night in Hong Kong, when he was twenty-four, he had a very bad road accident which, however, he survived.

'It was then that I knew I'd been spared and I decided to become a fortune-teller. God saved me, you see. This is the work I was meant to do and I do it. Several times I've tried to give it up, but it hasn't been allowed to me, so I go on. I try to help people with my knowledge, to put them on to the right roads. I'm a religious man in many ways. I believe in the gods and in spirits too and I've studied.'

Yip holds a collection of works on fortune-telling and the mysteries. For several generations, his family used to be known for giving hospitality and care to travelling monks and often these monks gave the family books. His father too collected books on fortune-telling, and it was from these that Yip gained his theoretical knowledge. 'But you need something else too – you would probably call it a sixth sense. It's a way of knowing things which isn't based on the learning in books, though that's necessary too.'

Most of his prognosis comes from his face-reading, with a little extra backup from the lines of the hands. He comments: 'People should know their fates. If it is good, there's nothing to fear. If it's bad, they can work to change it. That's where I can help them, you see.'

Reading the bones

Not practised so much in Hong Kong, but common in more traditional Taiwan, is the additional art of reading the bones. This was quite common in China in more ancient times and history records the case of a blind Taoist priest, Tao-shi, in the Tang Dynasty (780 – 805 AD) who became famous in this branch of knowledge. He foretold good and evil merely by feeling a person's bones, principally with reference to the length of the arm bones.

In Taiwan there is now a famous practitioner of this

distinctly more esoteric art, a blind man called Gwan Hsi who gently touches the hands of the person he is reading. From this touch he foretells the future.

This is called *Mo Ku*, or touch bones, and, despite the fact that its practitioners claim to relate it closely to the length and structure of the bones – so that it is therefore something of a physiological art – it seems, in fact, to come closer to divination. The fact that practitioners are often blind backs this up as a number of those involved in the divining arts are blind. Whether because it is a good way of making a living for a person so handicapped – blindness being a very low-status condition in traditional Chinese society – or whether because the blind are believed anyway to have special powers, is not clear. Certainly many Chinese are genuinely afraid of the blind.

I had the experience of walking along the street in Hong Kong one day behind a blind man tapping his way with a long stick and it was very obvious that older people – the more traditionally minded – were frightened by his approach. Many of them say that the tapping stick of the blind represents their communication with spirits. So the blind represent seers of a different kind.

It is clear that not only the blind but all fortune-tellers are somehow regarded as separate kinds of human beings – necessary but still separate – who deal in mysteries which most ordinary people are only too happy to leave to these supernatural experts.

9. The almanac

The traditional Chinese year is, as we have seen, calculated according to the lunar calendar, although officially all Chinese communities now use the solar calendar. Nevertheless, the important events of the year are always fixed according to the lunar calendar: the festivals, the ritual days and the organization of agricultural matters. The use of the lunar calendar is common throughout all rice-growing countries in Asia – India, Nepal, Thailand, Indonesia, China, Japan, Korea and so on – and the reason why is obviously connected with agriculture. The growing of rice and other crops in monsoon countries has more to do with lunar influences than solar. The ancients lived close enough to nature, the seasons and the stars to be aware of the interconnections, even if they did not have our own superb radio telescopes. This is why they recognize the importance of the moon over the sun in their daily affairs.

Being a rather pragmatic people, the Chinese then codified their knowledge even further and the result of all this, and much more, is to be found in the Chinese Almanac.

In Taiwan, they call it the Farmer's Almanac and in Hong Kong they call it the *Tong Sing*, the 'Know Everything Book' and they certainly do make an attempt to know everything. The variety of information contained in any one issue of the Almanac is quite astonishing and almost every Chinese household has one, though it is probably arguable how much they use it. Still, like the Bible in western households, the book is there, whether or not people actually read it.

In Hong Kong, for example, a population of some five million people snaps up one million copies of the Almanac each year – a figure which would make any publisher's mouth water – and a book which 20 per cent of the population buy must be considered significant by those people in some way.

The Almanac – whether in Taiwan or Singapore (where they like the Hong Kong copy best) or Hong Kong – is the one solid, traditional guide to all the information ordinary people need to live their lives fully, correctly and without offending the gods or the spirits. No fortune-teller, priest or diviner would ever be without it. It is probably the oldest continuous publication in the world, dating from about 2200 BC. The exact date is disputed by those to whom exact dates are very important. One tale says that it was the Emperor Yao in the year 2254 BC who ordered the seasons to be fixed so that farmers would know when to plant and when to harvest crops, though it is likely that the farmers would be able to work that one out for themselves. Still, the Chinese have a passion for writing everything down so that the words gain authority. Anyway, the story goes, Emperor Yao called together the country's best astrologers and mathematicians and put them to work on drawing up the first Almanac. From that time onwards – whenever it was – the entire nation was tied to this timetable, from the Emperor himself downwards. At first, it was a simple publication, just a crop-planting list for farmers. It was published annually by the Board of Astrologers and based on astrological data and observations from all over China.

All citizens had to abide by it on pain of death and this even applied to the Emperor himself. Traditionally, the Board of Astrologers prepared three versions of the Almanac, one specially handwritten for the sole use of the Emperor, a second for the Governors of the Provinces and the Heads of Vassal States and a third commonplace edition for everyone else. The only other difference was that, apparently, the Emperor's edition was more felicitously phrased, especially when it came to the bad news.

This publication ceased only in 1911 in China when the republic was established. However, in places where the community is largely Chinese, the Almanac is still printed every year. The format is still very like the original, a series of pages tied together complete with ancient woodblock illustrations; it is a publication of considerable charm. The Almanac is sold at traditional Chinese paper shops.

In its various editions, the Almanac contains a wealth of traditional information. Scholars who have spent years studying it comment that quite a number of sections contain information which is totally inaccurate now and that the text is often couched in Chinese which is not merely archaic, but, in a large number of instances, completely unintelligible. This is because the printing of the book is often undertaken, as it has been for centuries now, by those who have little scholarly knowledge of what they are dealing with. Given the exaggerated respect which the Chinese tend to have for the written word, and in particular the ancient written word, this nonsense has been passed down unchanged for a great many years. Regional variations have also arisen, especially since 1911, and there are wide differences of interpretation and text. In some instances the various editions cannot be reconciled at all.

However, despite this, the Almanac sells and sells. It

also costs very little to buy, which obviously has a lot to do with it. In Hong Kong, for example, the best edition of the Almanac, produced yearly by *fung shui* expert Choi Park-lai, still costs about two US dollars which makes it a tremendous bargain.

The largest section of the Almanac is an ancient text which does not change from year to year. Apart from the fact that it has been inadvertently altered by the ignorant, it is still presumably very much what it was four thousand years ago, even if some of that information is now unintelligible. This text contains all kinds of information useful for everyday life, even today. For example, both the Taiwanese and Hong Kong Almanacs contain large sections devoted to the writing of spells. There are spells for sickness, for driving away evil spirits, for headaches, for keeping away wild animals – a spell, charm or talisman for every problem likely to beset mankind, whether spiritual or secular. These are the same spells which the fortune-tellers and diviners write on pieces of yellow paper in the temples, which means that the ordinary man too could write out his own spells. Most do not, because they believe that the spell will only be as powerful as it need be if a real medium writes it out. Also, ordinary people do not want to get involved with supernatural forces. Nevertheless, the spells are there.

There are also sections on the interpretation of dreams, the significance of common phenomena, instructions for health problems and lists of herbal medicines for particular conditions, notes on baby care, help in choosing your child's name, astrological data, knowledge of the gods and deities and so on.

Some sections are really very intriguing. In the Farmer's Almanac from Taiwan, for example, there is one section entitled 'How to choose the sex of your child'. According to old traditions, there are several ways of ensuring that you get a child of the sex you want, which almost inevitably means a boy child. There is still enormous value attached to the birth of boys above that of girls, even in so-called egalitarian mainland China.

That probably also proves that the ancient wisdom concerning the begetting of boy children was not fool-proof, otherwise Chinese populations by now would be 90 per cent male, if parents could get their wishes for boy children!

However, for those who might like to try, here are a couple of ancient Chinese suggestions. The first method put forward is a slightly complex computation of numbers. It starts with a little Chinese rhyme which goes:

> *Chat chat say sap gau*
> *Man yau haw yut yau*
> *Choi hoi mo ling gung*
> *Joi go yat sap gau*

This translates as follows:

> Seven sevens are forty-nine
> Ask: 'Which is the pregnant month?'
> Take away the mother's age,
> Add nineteen.

It works like this. Let us assume a young woman, aged twenty, becomes pregnant in March (the third month of the year). Take forty-nine, add three (for March), total equals fifty-two. Subtract the woman's age, twenty, total equals thirty. An odd total means the child will be a boy, an even number means a girl. Therefore, to ensure the conceiving of a boy child, a little mathematical homework is necessary before the bedding-down takes place!

Yet another piece of ancient wisdom says that the way in which a couple makes love will influence the sex of the child. If they want a boy, the man should spend a long time on foreplay and restrain his own orgasm. For a girl, a man should enter a climax as soon as possible. The interesting thing about this is that it seems to recognize that it is the man who influences the sex of the child, which is a notion that most Asian peoples are resistant to accepting.

There is also the dieter's way of ensuring the choice of a child's sex. This involves both husband and wife eating the same kinds of food for seven days before they have intercourse. If they want to have a son, they must eat no meat for seven days. Instead, they must eat plenty of beancurd, carrots, cucumber, lettuce, potatoes, onions, mushrooms, macaroni, bananas, figs and drink plenty of milk. They must eat no pickles and no sour foods.

If, on the other hand, the couple want to have a girl child, they must eat plenty of meat – ham, beef, pork, chicken – and fish. They can also eat as many citrus fruits as they like, plus plenty of sour foods and pickles.

Both the Taiwanese and the Hong Kong Almanac deal extensively with the subject of dreams, for the Chinese regard dreaming as a serious matter. An early student of Chinese ways, Colonel Valentine Burkhardt, who wrote many newspaper articles about Chinese customs in Hong Kong in the 1930s, commented drily: 'The Chinese conception of dreams differs radically from the theories of Dr Freud', and indeed this is still true. Part of this important difference comes from the traditional beliefs about the soul. Although there is considerable diversity of opinion about the exact nature of the soul, most traditionalists agree on two things. The human body is possessed by two souls, one of a high spiritual nature known as the *hun* or *shen*, and the other of a low animal nature known as the *P'o*. The arguments begin when speculation moves into what happens to these spirits after death but, for the moment, we need not concern ourselves with this dispute, which has already been raging for several thousand years without being settled.

It is said that, at the moment of death, the higher spiritual essence, the *hun*, escapes through a hole at the top of the cranium and it is this same action which forms the basis of dreaming. When we dream, say the Chinese, the soul goes wandering about the world and all its encounters and adventures are as real as in everyday waking life, though we recall them as dreams when the soul returns and the body awakes from sleep. Therefore, there is no way that a Chinese can accept that his dreams are subjective or that their content has some deep psychological meaning to be divined. Incidentally, the time when the soul wanders abroad is regarded as very perilous, since the body is open to possession by spirits which could take over the body entirely and make it impossible for the soul to return. For the same reason, no one should ever be violently awakened in case the cord which joins body and soul be severed, leaving the spirit to wander homeless and therefore a threat to other humans. The human body left behind will be without reason or it may simply die: either way, the fate of a man separated from his essential spirit is not one to be envied.

Although the tradition does not accept the psychological significance of dreams, nevertheless there is a long and complex history of the divination of dreams, as their meaning is not necessarily clear to those who dreamed them. Even today there are many interpreters of dreams and, of course, there are many books which enable people to interpret the meaning of their own dreams in the absence of a suitable human aid. The importance of the interpretation of dreams has been long established, as the following story from the Shang dynasty illustrates.

It is said that the Emperor Wu Ting (accession 1324 BC) was in mourning for his father, upon whose help he had been very reliant. He had a dream in which the Gods of Heaven brought him an excellent minister of state. When he awoke he found he could recall the features of this minister with tremendous clarity. He summoned artists and described the man of his dream until they managed to produce a reasonable likeness. This he had copied and sent around the Empire until a man resembling the sketch could be found. Eventually, after much searching, he was. He was a humble labourer called Fu Yuet, but for all his lowly status, a man of considerable education and wisdom. The Emperor made him the chief minister of state and, so history tells us, he did his job well.

In another famous dream story, the great philosopher

Confucius dreamed that he saw a great mountain fall to the earth and when he woke he knew it was an intimation of approaching death. And there are other dreams which are considered to foretell death. For example, in Taiwan, people say that if you dream of losing your teeth or of snow falling, a parent will die. If a person says that he has dreamed that he was carrying a four-man litter, his family and friends will tell him to forget it, to think about it no longer, but they know that he will die.

According to the Almanac, the Chinese dream in categories. For example, there are the mountain and trees dreams, the kitchen utensil dreams, the silk dreams, the emperor dreams and so on, classifying all dreams according to the classical picture of Chinese society. Whether people still have emperor dreams, for example, when there is no longer an emperor to dream about, has not been established by research. Presumably being firm traditionalists, the Chinese are in fact still dreaming faithfully about emperors and mandarins according to the ancient rules.

The Almanac also contains an illustrated section on physiognomy and palm-reading, to help the reader judge men's characters from their appearance. The Taiwanese Farmer's Almanac has an additional section on the significance of the position of moles on the face, which is also considered to indicate the subject's fortune in life. All Almanacs have a wealth of Confucian quotes for every occasion to help readers become better members of society according to the classical tradition laid down by the Great Sage Confucius, whose life-task was the evolution of a correct view of society and the roles of human beings within it.

There is another on the significance of omens. For example, if the reader hears the cry of a crow between the hours of 3 a.m. and 7 a.m. from the south, it means that he will receive presents. If he hears the same cry, but at a different time, from 7 a.m. to 11 a.m., it means there will be wind or rain. Between 11 a.m. and 1 p.m., there will be quarrels. If a husband's ears itch between 11 p.m. and

1 a.m., there will be harmony between him and his wife. Between 1 a.m. and 3 a.m., a guest will soon be arriving and so on. There is an extensive list of such phenomena, some of it commonplace like tingling in the eyes or sneezing, and some of it somewhat archaic, like snuff forming on the wick of an oil lamp. It is really just another manifestation of the extreme concern for the future which the Chinese have displayed throughout their long history. Like the Ancient Romans and the Indians, they have always regarded omens as being of great significance: not only the phenomenon itself, but also the time at which it occurs.

The hours of the Chinese day are divided into periods of two hours each, which undoubtedly align with the western zodiac system in which the zodian signs dominate for two hours each through the periods of twenty-four hours. Each set of two hours is auspicious or not. Thus, there is not just one whole auspicious day, but a particular part of that day. That this is still considered of importance shows up in a number of ways. Even in Hong Kong, for example, a couple who are about to be married will consult a fortune-teller to find, not only the day, but also the auspicious hour at which they should embark on their married life. Days which are generally considered auspicious are crowded with marriages all over Hong Kong, while marriage rates drop severely during periods of inauspiciousness.

In fact, the greater part of the Almanac is given over to a detailed calendar which is the only section rewritten each year. It has to be written by someone very skilled in astrology, as each day must be divided up into the two-hour periods and auspicious and inauspicious times. Thus, a whole day is supplied with detailed instructions for the day's activities. A typical listing might be, for example, that a day is 'excellent for ritual ceremonies, praying, meeting friends, going on trips and getting married. Also good for moving house or opening a business. Don't distil wine today or hold a funeral service.' Another one goes: 'The right day to demolish your old house. Don't repair your kitchen or build a new oven today, but you can dig the earth and construct a drain. No haircut today!'

Most of the advice leans towards the agricultural, which of course is a reflection of traditional Chinese society as a largely agrarian one. There is also a great deal of information on the worship and appeasement of the dead, in addition to the fact that the first and the fifteenth day of every lunar month are regarded as excellent days for occult ceremonies of all kinds, which is why many occult festivals are held then.

Another popular section is that on numerology. The Chinese scholars – the alchemists and the magicians too – were always deeply involved with numerology and many of the concepts of Chinese numerology are shared with those of the Indians and the Babylonians, whom some experts regard as the possible innovators in the field. Much of the significance of numbers is, of course, both mystical and also associated with physics, as modern scholars, who study both the ancient tradition *I-Ching* and modern higher mathematics, are finding. But at street level a lot of superstitions about numbers have arisen. This is illustrated especially well in Hong Kong where superstition certainly has a great deal to do with some phenomena peculiar to the colony; good and bad numbers.

The element that makes numbers good or bad in Cantonese and Peking dialect is the punning and word-play possible in a many-toned language. It is also a big money game too. For example, in 1979 an anonymous Hong Kong businessman paid a reputed US$60,000 for a car number plate. The number? Six. Why? Because the number six and the word longevity are tone variations of the same basic word. Other fortunate numbers are two – easy; three – living or giving birth; eight – prosperity and nine – eternity. Combinations of numbers are also prized for their punning references to good luck and prosperity, the two issues most on the minds of the Cantonese. The good luck involved is also used in the names of businesses and clubs, to attract customers.

Bad numbers are one – the lonely number; four and seven – both death numbers. The number five can be bad luck in conjunction with certain other words. This can appear in rather novel ways. For example, Chin and Ng are both common Chinese surnames. Apart from this use, *chin* can also mean money and *ng* can mean no. Therefore, a man named *Chin* would, according to local opinion, be ill-advised to marry a woman surnamed Ng because together they would be *Ng Chin*, or 'No Money'. The endless ability of the Chinese in general, and the Cantonese in particular, to play the omen game with numbers and the sounds of words is truly inexhaustible, to an extent that can scarcely be appreciated by non-Chinese speakers.

The good/bad luck game with numbers as verbal puns actually has little to do with the classical system of numerology which is said to be a very metaphysical and mystical system, like that of the Jewish Kabbalah. For example, 108 is a mystical number of great spiritual significance and it therefore surfaces in a number of Chinese legends, although the storytellers now are unaware of its meaning. The number nine is another mystical number of power, and so it goes on.

Officialdom in Hong Kong pays silent respect to the Chinese beliefs connected with numbers. One thing the government does is to auction off auspicious car numbers each year, donating the proceeds to community services. From their beginning in 1973 to the end of 1980, a rather astonishing US$3 million had been raised by these auctions, which is quite a lot of car money in a territory of a mere 400 square miles, much of it not even suitable for cars. Another cunning official ploy is to run a number 88 bus to the racecourse, eighty-eight meaning 'double prosperity', which certainly brings the passengers crowding on in hopes of a winner.

A rather amusing section in the Hong Kong Almanac is the one in which the names of everyday objects are listed in Chinese and English with an approximate pronunciation guide. One look at this will explain the problems of bilingual communication in Hong Kong. For example, dried mushroom is pronounced 'do-lai-maa-si-laam', while husband is pronounced 'has-see-pang' and so on.

Not that the modern world is overlooked. Both the Taiwan and Hong Kong versions carry a section in which Chinese characters are given their number equivalent for the easy sending of telegrams in Chinese. A Chinese telegram arrives looking rather like this: '53 32 47 69 82' and so on, each number representing a particular written character.

Yes, there is something for every situation in the 'Know Everything' book.

10. The sweet and sour of etiquette

Whole oceans of misunderstanding flow between strangers when it comes down to matters of what each considers polite. This can be true even among those of the same nationality and ethnic group, and it is even more true when two entirely different cultures confront each other. Seldom is as much heat, anger and sheer contempt generated between foreigners as when they happen to disagree about what is good manners.

In Hong Kong, for example, this subject soon sets people at each other's throats. The Chinese of Hong Kong have the unenviable reputation, even among other Chinese, of being the rudest Chinese in the world, so much so that the Tourist Association has to run special campaigns to encourage workers in the tourist trade not to drive visitors away forever. Despite that, those foreigners hardy enough to survive daily life in the bristling little colony can still be amused from time to time by reading in the court reports about tourists unfortunate enough to have had ballpoint pens shoved up their nostrils by over-eager salesmen who resented their reluctance to buy.

It is worth pointing out that certain aspects of life among the Chinese simply do not carry the polite obligations of western society. For example, the Chinese, like most Asians, never queue for anything if they can manage not to and their eagerness to get on the bus, off the train or in the lift before everyone else is a rather natural reaction among the very poor who are in competition to get as high as they can as fast as they can. There are many millions of people in Asia all pushing for what they can get, knowing that if they hesitate, hundreds more will instantly be ahead of them. It is only the westerner, fortunate to come from a society rich enough to allow most people the confidence to know that there will be more – more buses, more trains, more food – who can afford to stand back for others. When a Chinese jumps ahead, it is not the personal act of aggression it would be in a westerner. An American or an Englishman could rightly take it as a deliberate violation for another person to take his taxi first, jump the queue ahead of him or push into a lift before he has managed to get out. In the West this is how we organize our society, even though there are many exceptions of course. This does not and could not work in Asia. All the wretched foreigner can do, for the sake of his blood pressure, is to try to understand that he is not the target.

When dealing with the Chinese there are a number of clichés which must instantly be discarded. The one about being silent and inscrutable, for example. Those who live among Chinese communities often joke about wishing that they were silent and inscrutable, but in fact they are loud, noisy and extremely scrutable. Among the Chinese in general and the Cantonese in particular – and it is the Cantonese who often make up the bulk of most overseas communities – noise is an absolute necessity for any festive occasion and the happier the celebration the noisier the celebrants. It was, after all, the Chinese who invented the fire-cracker, one way of marking jollities by a round of gunpowder going off like rifle fire. No, the only time when inscrutability is likely to creep into the occasion is when a *faux pas* too terrible to be acknowledged is committed, or during the first five visits to a local Chinese restaurant. The entirely sensible rationale behind this, according to Chinese thinking, is that you are not worth wasting warmth on until you have proved to be a faithful customer. The idea of showing warmth in order to encourage the customer to return is simply not a Chinese concept, nor a part of the everyday psychology working among the Chinese.

Much is made of the concept of face, which is often said to be uniquely Chinese. While it is certainly true that pride is of great importance to the Chinese, it is equally important to many other ethnic groups and nationalities and is often overplayed by those who may know the Chinese but obviously do not know other cultures in which pride is equally valued. There can surely be no one in the world who would wish to be publicly admonished, humiliated or otherwise made to feel small and unimportant. It is true that the face game can be very deviously played among the Chinese, so that outsiders can be made to lose face in the eyes of every Chinese present without being aware of it themselves. It is, however, questionable that a person has lost pride if he himself does not actually think so. Pride, like most 'self' concepts, is largely in the heart of its possessor.

The friendliest meal can be a face game of tedious nuances. Who sits in the place of honour, who picks up the chopsticks first, who gives the choicest morsels to whom, who pays the bill. And the final piece of face, one which westerners find most objectionable, the public announcement of the bill total so that all the guests know exactly what was paid for them – just the opposite of what sophisticated western diners would expect.

Methods of greeting

As food is perhaps the most important thing in the world to a Chinese it is not surprising to find that the normal greeting between people in the morning is:

'Have you eaten your rice yet?'

To which the answer must be: 'Yes, thank you.' Even if it is not true. It is the exact equivalent of the English greeting: 'How are you?' and the reply, 'Fine, thanks.'

If greeting a long-lost Chinese friend of the same sex, you are permitted to pat his arm in a friendly fashion, but any attempt to hug may well cause an attack of inscrutability to break out. Most Chinese men are quite good at shaking hands these days, but Chinese women on the whole still do it with an air of faint distaste which should not be taken personally. The greeting bow has more of less passed out of fashion, although a half-hearted attempt at it can be seen among older Chinese, but hand-shaking has not become totally acceptable. Everyone does it but without enthusiasm. Beware the Chinese man who looks you firmly in the eye and shakes your hand with a warm muscular crunch: he has learned his stuff at a Dale Carnegie course and wants to sell you something.

When Chinese introduce themselves, names often cause confusion. In Hong Kong, where bilingualism has not really arrived, the Chinese often have their business cards printed in English but with names in the Chinese order. So a man who presents a card reading Wong Wing Chan may be Mr Chan, as westerners would expect, or may be Mr Wong. The Chinese style is to put the family name first, followed by the given name and finally the middle name. Most men will elect to be called by their surname alone or maybe by their initials. They usually dislike foreigners getting their names wrong and to avoid the problem altogether will take on an English-style name. Although this practice seems a very colonial one, in fact the Chinese do tend to change their names throughout life. They have a family name, a school name and so on, which is why they sometimes seem to bear an almost sinister number of different names. They are reluctant to give personal names to non-Chinese-speaking foreigners because in English they cannot have the normal polite prefix that is attached to personal names. Our Mr Wong, for example, has two personal names, Wing and Chan. His close friends would probably address him in Chinese as Ah-Chan, which serves the same kind of purpose as the attachment of San to a Japanese name. The best thing to do when confronted with these problems is simply to ask. Of course, you will lose face, but then there are so many ways in which this can happen anyway that it does not really matter.

As an extra clue many Chinese now have their names written in English in the following way: Wong Wing Chan. Then you know the surname is Wong, the given name Chan and the middle name Wing.

Chinese women frequently retain their maiden names and you should not be too surprised if Mr Wong says: 'I'd like you to meet my wife, Miss Tam.'

Shopping

When shopping, there are a few things a customer should be aware of, if he does not want to ruin the shopkeeper's day. The first thing is that, in common with other Asian shopkeepers, the Chinese attach special importance to the first customer of the day because they believe he sets the style for the day's business. So, if you want to get a really good price from a Chinese merchant, then you should be first in the shop so that he will offer you an advantageous rate in order to make a sale and bring good fortune for the day. You really should purchase something if you are the first, even if it is just a small token of your willingness to buy. In Singapore and Malaysia, the most traditional shopkeepers will take a bucket of water and throw it into the street, if their first customer fails to buy, to wash away the bad luck that will otherwise mar their day of business.

Gifts

The whole arrangement of giving gifts is somewhat reversed among the Chinese, when compared with western habits. For example, a present is likely to be greeted with 'Oh, no, you shouldn't,' which basically can be interpreted as, 'Well, I'm glad you did but I hope you don't think I'm greedy enough to have expected it of you.' Presents for Chinese friends should be wrapped in red or gold paper as blue and white are the colours of mourning and grief. Once you have given your present, a Chinese recipient will then put it to one side to be opened privately later. It is considered bad manners to open a gift in front of the giver, quite the opposite behaviour from our own. It is also considered inappropriate to be too effusive in thanking someone for a gift – that is all part of the face game too, not to show eagerness for something free.

Usually when a stranger is visiting a family for the first time, he does not take any gifts. He certainly does not take food or drink, as is common among most westerners. To the Chinese this would imply that you thought he did not have enough food and drink to offer you himself, which, of course, would mean loss of face yet again. It would also have the added connotation that you were trying to buy your way into the family. However, at the third visit or so, it is permitted to take a gift. For good luck, such gifts should never be given singly. One is a lonely number in Chinese culture and therefore unlucky. So, an ideal gift could be two boxes of sweets or an even number of other things – maybe six or eight peaches. When you leave the house, the host may return two of the peaches, for example, which is his way of returning to you some of the good luck you have brought him.

When visiting a Chinese family, all the entertaining will be done in the family living-room. The Chinese seldom succumb to the western oddity of showing strangers all over the house. They think this a very curious way of behaving. Historically, some people attribute this reticence to the still fairly common practice of keeping large amounts of money around the house, which might well be true. But it is also likely to be connected with face again. Certain rooms are kept for display and the living-room is one of them. Others are not.

If you are lucky enough to be staying with a Chinese family, most of the normal rules of polite behaviour apply exactly as they would with a family of any other race. While advisors on etiquette in Singapore mention that it is quite unacceptable for a woman to wash and leave her underwear out to dry – such wantonness! – in Hong Kong this is not likely to be true. The best thing is to check with the lady of the house, or some younger member, what you should do about your washing. It is true that, even in more down-to-earth Hong Kong, women seldom hang their more frivolous bits of underwear outside where strangers can see them and presumably be inspired with licentious thoughts. Old ladies in Hong Kong think it brings bad luck to walk under a washing-line bearing women's underwear.

There are a number of apparently normal things that a visitor should never bring as gifts to a Chinese family, usually because of their associations or because it is felt that they would bring bad luck. Among some Chinese, for example, a stork is a symbol of a woman's death. This applies largely among people of the Hokkien-speaking group. It would be a very unfortunate move to send a new baby greeting card with a stork on it to such a woman, as she would certainly think it a bad omen at the very least. As there are plenty of other cards to send on these occasions, if in doubt avoid all risk of offending. As it happens, the stork among most Cantonese is identified as a symbol of longevity, not of death. Even so, as none of the Chinese subscribe to the theory that babies are brought by storks anyway, the significance of such a card is likely to be wasted. The Chinese know that in reality babies are brought by boat from heaven, the divine cargo arranged according to sex. When the maternity wards of Hong Kong see a lot of baby boys arriving, the nurses are likely to joke about the boys' boat arriving from heaven.

One gift that no non-Chinese speaker would be aware of as a frightening omen is a clock. The Cantonese word for clock has a homophone which means 'to go to a funeral' and so to give anyone a clock as a gift can be construed as a bad sign. Similarly, gifts should not be white, blue or black in colour, as these are mourning colours. The Hong Kong Cantonese, and perhaps others, also make the same associations with colours which come near to these hues, such as green and purple.

Never give sharp objects, such as scissors or knives, which could symbolize the cutting off of a friendship.

Flowers are not often given as gifts among the Chinese. Usually, they are given to the sick or, even worse, sent to funerals. They used never to be given in greeting, though this is changing and certainly in Hong Kong where expensive flowers are now considered acceptable as a pleasant enough present. One thing to observe when giving flowers to a Chinese is that the number of the flowers must never be uneven. The favourite dozen roses of the British would be welcome, but the five roses of the French and Germans would be regarded as unmitigated disaster doubled – once for the gift of flowers and twice for the bad luck brought by odd numbers.

That old standby present – a handkerchief – would certainly ruin the day for a traditional Chinese, to whom they represent mourning. Handkerchiefs are frequently given to mourners at funerals.

Eating etiquette

Many of the rituals of etiquette are reserved for that most sacred of occasions for the Chinese – eating. Food is the poetry and passion of the Chinese, especially perhaps of the Cantonese whose obsessive greed is explained by the years of famine and suffering which have certainly marred their long and turbulent history. It is in eating that people are most likely to come into contact with the Chinese, so it is as well to be aware of the politenesses of the table.

To begin with some generalities. The more courses there are in a Chinese dinner, the more honour is being paid to the guests. A typical western-style setting of three courses could be misunderstood by Chinese who were not familiar with the habit. A further hint if entertaining the Chinese is never to serve dairy dishes or cheese if there are alternatives. Although dietary habits are changing, many older people cannot digest milk and milk products. This is because it was never traditional to include milk in the human diet after the weaning of a baby and the enzymes particularly associated with the digestion of milk disappear once they no longer seem to be needed. Therefore suddenly to reintroduce milk later on is to load the stomach with a food which it is no longer equipped to deal with and stomach upsets or diarrhoea can easily result. This does not apply when people have continued to drink milk, as is common among youngsters today in Singapore and Hong Kong. Perhaps for the same reason, or may be it is just a cultural taste, many people dislike cheese – a distaste common among many Asians, not just the Chinese.

The question of drink at meals is also a completely different one among the Chinese. Traditionally, they rarely used to drink anything other than tea with their food and this is still commonly considered to be the best accompaniment. There is a widely held belief – now supported by medical evidence in the West – that the iced drinks so beloved of Americans are very bad for the digestion. They freeze the digestive process temporarily, making it hard for the stomach enzymes to get down to digestion. However, status and drink have become associated in the minds of many modern Chinese and a new favourite among the men – less so among the women – is the finest French brandy which is then quite destroyed by the addition of a soft drink such as Seven Up. Sadly, this appalling mixture is the usual accompaniment to Chinese food among those who can afford it in Singapore and Hong Kong, less so in traditional Taiwan.

Usually Chinese tea is served throughout a meal and it is a useful way for people to show courtesy to each other by the small attention of topping up the surrounding cups or glasses. The polite guest always tops up those around him before doing it to his own. Among the Hong Kong Chinese, instead of thanking each other for the courtesy, they tap the two first fingers of the right hand twice on the table. It is said that this polite gesture came about when one of the Emperors took to wandering incognito among his people. The courtiers who accompanied him could not carry out any of the usual ritual politenesses towards his Imperial Majesty without blowing his cover, so they devised the discreet little two-fingered gesture of thanks now used by most Hong Kong Chinese. When you are served with tea, apart from the acknowledgment, you are also supposed to drink some. Even if you do not wish to drink it, it is obligatory to take a sip or two to show willing.

As most people are aware, the Chinese dining table is round, so that no one can be up or down table and therefore lose face. The most honoured guests usually sit beside the host, who himself sits with his face to the door – presumably so that he can watch for Triad Society members rushing in with choppers and protect his guests accordingly. In Singapore and Malaysia the side of honour is the left hand of the host, but this is not rigidly so in Hong Kong. Whichever side the honoured guest is on, one of the marks of honour will be choice little titbits placed in the bowl or on the plate before him and he will eat these with all due enthusiasm, or else!

It is usual for the diners to utter exclamations of surprise and delight when the dishes arrive on the table. From the Chinese, with their wonderful enthusiasm for food, these exclamations are usually totally sincere, but even the most uptight westerner is supposed to raise an exclamation or two and to praise the flavours and the appearance of the food. Remember that, after all, the host did not simply tick these dishes off on a menu. Most Chinese use the menu as a mere aid to much more detailed discussion about the food and how it should be cooked and what is good that day and so on. So the complete meal is the result of considerable plotting between the host and the waiter or cook.

When the proceedings are really ready to get going, the host usually signals this by raising his glass. Notice how this is done, because you should imitate it. The left hand holds the glass, the fingers of the right hand support it and both lift it high as a greeting to all the guests and a signal to start the fun. If the host or other guests during the dinner call out 'Yum sing', then be prepared to drain your glass bottom up, because that is what it means.

When the food arrives, the host usually again indicates the start of the meal by taking up his chopsticks. There is no secret method of using chopsticks. Just as there is no secret Italian method of eating spaghetti tidily, the Chinese use chopsticks to get food into their mouths almost any old how they can. Watch a Hong Kong Chinese literally shovel the rice into his open mouth with the sticks and you will see instantly that there is no finely refined method to this manoevring.

No, the politenesses of chopsticks are merely not to use them to take the biggest piece of food on the dish nor the last piece (loss of face). The dish is usually placed on a turntable device which enables everyone to help himself. Never lift the dish off the table, even to help someone else to get at the food. It is considered bad manners, just as reaching over someone else's chopsticks is also bad manners.

Soup needs a spoon and chopsticks. The chopsticks are for the solid pieces and the spoon should be wielded towards you, not away in the Western style. If you can manage a noise approximating to an enthusiastic slurping, so much the better. Another contrast to western dining habits is to abandon the pieces you cannot eat. The bones and the shells should be removed by using chopsticks and then placed on the table beside you. A waiter will then clear them away. You can try to balance them on your plate but you may end up with no space for the actual food.

A big dinner has many courses. There could be up to twelve of them and you are supposed to have something from each one, so remember this when you start out and take things steadily. If your hosts offers you more, refuse first or you will look greedy and lose face. Just a morsel or two will do to signal acceptance. To place chopsticks down beside your bowl signals repletion and the end of eating.

Although there is little agreement on the aesthetics of wielding chopsticks and, in Hong Kong anyway, often precious little in the way of aesthetics to be seen in the average restaurant, there are certain things you must not do with them. You must never wave them or point them at people. Neither must you jokingly stick them upright in the rice bowl, or even rest them like that momentarily. A severe attack of inscrutability is likely to break out around the table since the Chinese see this as a reminder of the ceremonies for the dead; it echoes the upstanding joss stick which is burned for the spirits of the dead.

Burping enthusiastically is a sign of appreciation for the meal, but you do not necessarily have to follow suit.

One definite don't: don't turn over a fish on a plate, not even to get the flesh off it. This is considered a bad omen, especially if there are any sailors or fishermen present as it represents the capsizing of a boat.

Although the Chinese often drag meals out interminably, once the food is finished they all get up and go home. There are no after-meal lingerings such as is normal among westerners. A proper Chinese restaurant will not even have any coffee to serve you, only another glass of tea to speed you on your way. Neither will a traditional Chinese restaurant have fortune cookies – they are an American invention.

There are some courtesies amongst the Chinese which

westerners sometimes find startling. Men are usually served first. After all, not only are they far more important, they are also expected to be paying the bill. In the same way, if you are a woman, do not expect a Chinese man to open a door for you or draw your chair out for you. He just might, if he has had a western education, but do not wait for those little attentions. The meal could be over before you get them!

Babies

Chinese attitudes are somewhat divided over babies these days. Traditionally, it was always considered to be very bad luck to draw the attention of evil spirits to young babies. Even today, nearly all babies wear little wristlets or anklets of jade or precious metal to keep spirits away from them. And it is not long since the Hakka people used to call their babies ugly names like Piggie and Little Dog, to suggest to the spirits that these were not desirable little human cherubs but nasty little animals. So, a certain schizophrenia occurs about babies. Most mothers appreciate a certain amount of attention to their babies but would start to feel uncomfortable if it became too effusive, as there are still lingerings of unease about this.

There are many more subtleties of good manners but the main thing, as with good manners the world round, is sincerity of heart. The Chinese are very acutely percep-tive of feelings – some would describe them as being a very psychic people in some ways – and they always appreciate kindliness and good will and can understand it when they meet it, even if language itself cannot express it.

11. Food and drink: harmony fuel

The one great passion shared by virtually all Chinese is their love of good food and that, of course, means Chinese food. This enthusiasm is shared by many people all over the world who are not Chinese. In fact, it is probably true to say that the one ethnic cuisine which can be found everywhere is Chinese. Whether in Macau or Madagascar, in Fiji or Tibet, the traveller can be certain of finding a little Chinese restaurant tucked away in some small street at which he can eat familiar food. It is just unfortunate that what many people think of as being typically Chinese is really nothing of the sort. Sweet and sour sauce and chop suey have as much to do with traditional cooking as pizza does with Italian cooking. They are scornful immigrant inventions concocted for those who know no better.

The Chinese are very serious about their eating. As I have suggested, they are positively obsessed by food in a way which speaks eloquently about the long years of famine and deprivation that have scarred China's history;

and they also take many more things into consideration when cooking than a mere mixture of pleasant-tasting ingredients. They consider not only the look, texture and flavour of the food, but also its other properties: its medicinal powers, its inherent harmony and the way in which it affects the body's own harmony, the balance of *yin* and *yang*.

Far from dropping things carelessly into a wok, the Chinese cook is working from a long history which makes food the subject of a complex alliance between nutritional science and philosophy. It may be hard to equate this rather grandiose statement with the offerings of an average Chinese take-away in the United States or Britain and even harder to associate it with the fat stallholder wiping his greasy fingers on his vest while he tosses noodles over a fire at the side of a Hong Kong street. But, of course, the point is that much of the information which he applies will have been automatically absorbed from childhood. Just as certain westerners swear by the healing and soothing qualities of chicken broth, without submitting the evidence to laboratory testing, in the same way the Chinese do things because they merely accept that it is so. Therefore, any Chinese mother will treat her little boy's cold by making him eat dried orange peel – either salted or crystallized; usually the former – knowing that this will do him good. The fact that science has in recent years confirmed that the peel of the orange contains the highest concentration of vitamin C in the entire fruit concerns her not at all. She knows that grandmother always treated colds thus and undoubtedly her granddaughter will one day do the same.

In the latter decades of the twentieth century, many traditional medical practices have been investigated, instead of merely being pooh-poohed, and found to contain convincing evidence of a real scientific basis. A very simple illustration of this can be given from English country tradition. In days gone by, country folk used to treat infected cuts and wounds by laying a cobweb over them to help the healing process. Bizarre though this seemed at first to the highly technical medical science of our day, investigation after the Second World War revealed that cobwebs, for whatever reason, contained a high concentration of natural penicillin. Another rural practice was to smear an infected cut or wound with honey and there are still many people who do this for their own pet animals. Again, laboratory investigation has shown that honey possesses its own antibiotic, which is undoubtedly why it has so long been advocated as a good restorative for a sore throat.

In the same way, when we look at a number of Chinese beliefs about the properties of food and drink, we should perhaps be cautious about regarding them as mere superstitions. Some traditional beliefs have already been confirmed through the analysis of food and drink and possibly many more remain to be confirmed. As an example of this, we have the story of a particular fungus which the Chinese add to certain dishes, claiming that it is a cleanser of the blood. Investigation by western scientists has shown that the fungus – commonly found in Taiwan and in certain parts of China – seems to have a definite effect on the build-up of cholesterol in the blood. The clues which led to this investigation and its rather exciting conclusion came out of a medical realization that a certain sector of a Chinese population seemed to have a remarkably low incidence of coronary thrombosis compared with the rest of their compatriots. The factor responsible for this was traced to the frequent use of a particular white fungus in their diet – the only dietary and environmental difference.

As with many other aspects of their culture, the Chinese look for harmony in cooking and eating. The harmony must come, not only from the ingredients themselves, but from the temperament of the eater and his food, the relationship of both with the time and the season of the year and even the requirements of the moment. If, for example, a man needs a lot of fire and energy, he will seek to eat the foods which give that, rather than foods which will soothe and still his spirit. When all these different elements have reached harmony, then *yin* and *yang* are considered to be in balance.

All foods are classified as belonging to one of three categories. They are heating or *yang*, cooling or *yin*, or neutral. The meaning of the terms heating and cooling is not immediately obvious as it is not necessarily anything to do with the temperature of the food nor with its spiciness. Rather, it is the effect it has on the body system and its *yin-yang* balance. Heating foods add *yang* to the body system, cooling foods add *yin* and how much this affects the eater will depend on his own natural state of *yin* and *yang*, which is a very individualistic matter. Being *yin* or *yang* is an amoral condition. There is no good or bad attached to either; and it is also a variable state. It is sometimes hard for the non–Chinese fully to understand these terms because basically the vocabulary is unfamiliar, as are the concepts behind the words. Sometimes, when we look at Chinese theories of medicine and health, we are rather in the position of South Sea Islanders listening to Captain Cook explaining the mysteries of the navigational compass. We hear the words but we do not really understand and neither do we see why it is necessary, when we can steer so well by the stars and the waves.

Even the vocabulary can be confusing. For example, the Chinese regard water melon as heating, not cooling. Alcohol can be either heating or cooling – brandy is heating, but beer is cooling. Hot tea, on the other hand, can be heating or cooling according to its type. And so on.

Therefore, when the Chinese chef plans a menu he looks for harmony, rather than counting the proteins or the calories. However, it often works out just right in the end because food put together according to the principles of harmony is usually nutritionally sound as well. After all, it was the Chinese who invented the stir-fried vegetables cooked quickly in order to preserve the vitamins, even though they had never heard of vitamins.

It was also the Chinese who very long ago said that too much meat was bad for the bowels. The Chinese did not, however, say it caused cancer of the bowels – they said that too much red meat is too *yang*, too heating for the bowels. It is perhaps not too fanciful to regard cancer as the product of an overheated system, since the Chinese equate heat with activity. Here is another example of looking more closely at the vocabulary of a different culture and seeking our equivalent for it, rather than regarding it as quaint because it does not correspond exactly with our own word usage. It is also useful to remember that, after all, with their passionate interest in food, the Chinese have a long history of observing the results of eating it and drawing valid conclusions from their observations.

Even as far back as the Chou Dynasty (1122 – 249 BC), court dieticians were appointed to plan the imperial banquets with due regard to the seasons of the year, the properties of the food and the *yin-yang* principles of harmony. These dieticians would also consider very carefully the physical types they were dealing with – whether the eater was a *yang* type, a *yin* type or a mixture of the two.

To do this, observation of the person concerned would be necessary and the human types analysed then are still those of today. A very active outgoing person is considered to be a *yang* person, a quiet introvert is *yin* and a nervous or changeable person is a *yin-yang* mixture. These types are all modified by their illnesses and by what they eat. For example, a nice, quite amenable *yin* type could well become rather *yang* if he suffered from a liver disease which would cause a *yang* imbalance. He will then be characterized by the irascible, short-tempered behaviour we have come to regard as 'liverish'. Such a sufferer would be put on a *yin* diet which would help to counteract that fiery *yang* and, interestingly enough, we would find that diet remarkably similar to the diet which a western doctor would give his liver patients. By a different route, the same destination can be reached.

The point of all this is to make sure that the body's supply of *chi* is ensured. *Chi* is a word with many meanings, or perhaps one central meaning with many aspects. It could most easily and loosely be translated as energy and the concept of *chi* seems to refer to a specific energy unit, rather than the abstract idea of energy. The problem for westerners is that we have not yet discovered the way to measure *chi*, as we have discussed, which does not worry the Chinese but does disturb all those doctors and scientists who come up against the word in almost every aspect of Chinese medicine, acupuncture, martial arts, earth science and so on. Good food, say the Chinese, increases *chi* and that is what body harmony is all about. When *chi* is plentiful and flowing along *chi* channels (the meridians of acupuncture), the body is healthy. Therefore, food feeds *chi*. Blocked *chi* leads to sickness and problems of temperament, both an inherent part of the whole harmonized body.

Certain types of people need certain kinds of food to balance their *yin* and *yang* and enable their *chi* to flow energetically round the system. Therefore, we must eat according to our type, say the Chinese. Fat but active people are *yang* types and to keep their balance they must eat *yin* foods, especially plenty of vegetables. They must not drink coffee or heating teas, nor eat spices which will put their *yang* into overdrive and and make them hyperactive.

On the other hand, thin and active people are also *yang* types but suffer from inadequate *chi* which makes them temperamental and subject to extreme swings of mood. Such people have to avoid increasing this imbalance by eating too many sugary or salty foods. They need plenty of vegetables (*yin*) and must avoid the rich foods which their unbalanced systems make them yearn for. Cravings for certain kinds of food are commonly the result of imbalance in *yin* and *yang* and, of course, lead to further ill-health.

On the other side of the scale come the *yin* people.

Firstly, there are the fat and sluggish types with poor metabolisms, sensitive to cold and often suffering from digestive troubles. They need to eat foods which help their digestive systems, such as the organ meats (heart, liver, kidneys, intestines and brains). The Chinese believe that to eat a particular organ has a beneficial effect on the same organ in the eater, hence all the exotic kinds of penis which males are supposed to eat. This may sound like sympathetic magic, but perhaps when we consider that in this century it has been discovered that eating quantities of liver helps sufferers from liver conditions, we might do well to hold our scepticism in check for a while longer. Fat, sluggish types are also allowed to eat the stimulating foods which *yang* types long for but are forbidden to have and they are encouraged to take a little alcohol to help their sluggish circulation along.

The saddest sufferer of all is thought to be the thin and sluggish person. This type has a serious lack of *chi* energy to draw upon and therefore suffers from a weakness of all major organs, as well as being in fragile health generally. They must avoid cooling foods and eat plenty of vegetables, well-cooked to remove the cooling effects. Hot and stimulating foods should be their staple diet and plenty of ginger ought to be added in cooking. The term 'to ginger up' has a real meaning in Chinese cooking.

Nervous and active types are considered by the Chinese to suffer from inadequate circulation, both of blood and of *chi* energy. Because of this, they tend to suffer digestive problems and fatigue. They are supposed to avoid stimulating foods or food which would particularly upset their digestive systems. This includes beans and cabbage which form gas in the bowels, as well as onions, pork and chillies. Instead, they must eat raw and lightly cooked vegetables, seaweeds and citrus fruits and certain very beneficial seafoods, such as clams, scallops and abalone.

The final category is the nervous inactive person, who suffers from poor digestion and sluggish internal organs. This makes their health unsteady and leads to easy fatigue. To counteract these, they must eat the same kinds of foods as nervous and active types, with the addition of extra salt to fight the tendency to fatigue. They are not to eat toast or roasted meats and fish, which are irritants to their nervous systems.

Of course, such is the range of human possibility that it is not easy to envisage everyone fitting clearly into one of these categories. Many people show signs of being more than one type, or change from one to another owing to changes of circumstances, health, conditions, environment and so on. But the ancient Chinese did regard this as covering the range of possibilities, even if many people were not obviously members of one class. Today, the Chinese still consider these the basic classifications of human types and therefore see the careful choosing of diet as essentially relating to the needs of that type. They still eat to seek this balance. Thus, a man aware of having too much *yang* energy in his body will choose cooling foods to balance this. In the winter, it is normal to concentrate on *yang* foods which increase the body's heat, while *yin* foods will be the choice for the height of summer. This is also something which westerners do, without seeing their choice of foods and drinks in these vocabulary terms.

Accepting the relationship of food and temperament, the next logical step is one which is familiar to the Chinese – that of changing your temperament by what you eat. While it is accepted that your type cannot be totally changed, nevertheless there is a great possibility of considerable modification. A person who suffers from too much *yang* energy is often hot-tempered and, to control this, he must avoid further heating foods. If, however, he continues to eat fatty meats, fried foods, eggs, drink liquor and smoke cigarettes, these will create an uncontrollable temper.

It is quite usual for parents to take children to traditional Chinese doctors to consult over their temperaments, so much is this recognized as a body-mind factor, not merely a choice of behaviour. One doctor in

Hong Kong tells of two exhausted parents who brought their six-year-old son with them.

'Oh doctor,' they wailed, 'he's so badly behaved! We don't know what to do with him.'

Sure enough, the child was badly behaved. He bit the doctor who tried to examine him, lay on the floor and shrieked with rage, tore up the newspapers and generally behaved like a totally spoiled brat.

But the doctor realized, on examining the boy, that he was suffering from extreme *yang*, a general overheating of the whole system due to a faulty diet. The boy was a junk food addict, loved to eat greasy crisps and drink sugar-loaded soft drinks, as well as eating a lot of meat and fried foods.

'What I had there,' said the doctor afterwards, 'was an overheated little monster!'

So he instructed the parents to put the child on a strictly cooling diet. Plenty of vegetables, no meat, nothing fried, no sweet drinks, plenty of fruit, no spices and so on. Within two weeks, the child's temper had cooled considerably and he was no longer subject to the extremes of rage which had made them bring him to the doctor.

The same doctor did the opposite with a dog. A friend lived out in Hong Kong's rural New Territories. Due to the influx of illegal immigrants coming over the border from China, he decided to get a good guard-dog in order to warn his family when intruders were about. Many of the other villagers had had their houses broken into by the desperate new arrivals from China on the lookout for money to line their bare pockets and the man did not want this to happen to his family. So he bought an Alsatian puppy.

A few weeks later the doctor went out to the village to visit his friend. The dog rushed up to him and greeted him with frantic waves of his tail.

'Nice dog,' commented the doctor.

'Yes, that's just the problem,' said his friend gloomily. 'He treats everyone like that. He's completely useless as a

guard dog. I think I'm going to have to get rid of him –
and he cost me a lost of money!'

'Don't do that,' said the doctor. 'Give him to me and
I'll turn him into a guard-dog for you.'

He took the dog home and changed his diet totally,
concentrating on giving the animal plenty of heating
foods. At the end of the week, he returned one newly
fierce Alsatian to its delighted owner. And, of course,
what can be done for an Alsatian, can be done for a
human being. Those who would like to develop control
over easily lost tempers or who would like to speed up
their own rather sluggish systems might like to experiment a little for themselves with the Chinese way of
balancing the system. Here are some guidelines for the
most common foods.

Very heating: Beef, butter, chicken fat, chillies, choco-
late, coffee, curry, dog meat, fish (smoked), lamb,
onions, peanut butter, peanuts (roasted), pepper (black),
pork (fat), whisky

Heating: Cheese, chicken (liver), eggs, garlic, pepper
(green), goose, ham, kidney beans, leeks, pig's liver,
potato, rabbit, sugar (brown), sunflower seeds, turkey,
walnuts, wine

Very cooling: Banana, beansprouts, clams, crab,
cucumber, kelp, mung beans, mussels, peppermint
leaves, root beer, shrimps, soda water, Seven-Up,
soyabean milk, tea (chrysanthemum, green)

Cooling: Almonds, apple, asparagus, bamboo, barley,
beer, broccoli, cabbage, celery, Coca Cola, corn, duck,
eel, fish, grapes, honey, ice cream, lemonade,
mushrooms, oranges, oysters, pineapple, salt, spinach,
strawberries, sugar (white), tofu (beancurd), tomatoes,
cold water

Neutral foods: These can be eaten in large quantities
without affecting the balance of *yin* and *yang* in the body.
They include: beans (red and string), bread, carrots,
cauliflower, cherries, chicken (meat), dates, milk,

peaches, peas, pigeon, plums, raisins, rice (brown), rice (steamed white), and hot water among others.

In addition to these categories, there is another way of classifying food, according to its nourishing qualities. When a Chinese feels in need of the extra boost such foods give, he will add it temporarily and usually sparingly to his diet.

Lightly nourishing: Abalone, beef steak, carrots, cat, cow's milk, garlic, goat's milk, honey, kidney beans, lamb's hearts and kidneys, Ovaltine, scallops, spinach, wine (grape, rice)

Moderately nourishing: Chicken, dog, duck, eel, frog's legs, lamb, fish roe, oxtail, quail's eggs, rabbit

Very nourishing: Bird's nest soup, chicken soup with herbs, ginseng tea, pigeon, pig's liver, wine (herbal)

It is quite hard for the uninformed observer to find the common link between each of these foods which makes them nourishing in Chinese eyes. Some, it is true, are high-protein foods, but others are somewhat puzzling – the inclusion carrots, for example. The decision about nourishing foods seemed to be linked to their scarcity value. Just as westerners have a preference for special foods when they are in fragile health, the Chinese too like to have foods which in the past have been associated with luxury. In famine-torn China, high protein foods featured all too rarely on the table of most Chinese families and for that reason alone they are treasured for their real or imagined qualities of value as a food source.

One Chinese scholar makes the point that the value of certain of the foods relates directly to traditional beliefs about them. For example, people commonly believe that rather gelatinous foods have a very high protein content; hence bird's nest soup, shark's fin soup, fish lips and sea slugs are all regarded as special treats. There is thought to be a connection between the human body and these foods. The rather slimy quality of many of them when cooked is precisely what appeals to a Chinese, especially a man, who equates it with sperm fluid. By eating such foods, he believes that he is enhancing his sexual prowess. There are also many traditional beliefs about the special powers of human saliva and, before we dismiss them, we should recall that scientists have lately discovered a factor in animal saliva which speeds up the healing of cuts and wounds when they are licked. Whether such healing factors really exist in these foods has not yet been explored.

Very nourishing foods, incidentally, are only supposed to be taken in modest quantities or the body will become unbalanced again.

Just as most of the above foods have special healing abilities, there are also irritants which hold up healing. These are referred to as irritating, wet and poisonous foods. If irritating, they inhibit the healing of wounds, broken limbs and even cause skin allergies. Wet foods are those which cause infection in wounds and poisonous foods are particularly bad for those who suffer from weak internal organs or low *chi*.

Mild irritants: Asparagus, beef, bread, carrots, clams, fish roe, garlic, ginseng, goosemeat, leeks, mustard, onions, pineapples, potato, turnip, whisky, wine
Severe irritants: Aubergines, crabs, lobsters, shrimps, vinegar

Interestingly, some of these foods are known for their role as triggers for allergy sufferers. Most of them, however, are only regarded as irritants in someone whose health is already somewhat fragile. For example, when I was suffering from a broken arm in Hong Kong, waiters in restaurants would point out that there were foods I must not order if I wanted my arm to heal well. Traditional lore about food is obviously common knowledge.

There is also a long history of occult practices connected with food, many of them associated with the Taoist search for longevity or even immortality. Like the alchemists of the West, who had, in fact, a shorter history than those of China, the search for the ultimate turned from metaphor to reality when the alchemists began to try to manufacture a food or drink which would make them immortal.

The legendary Emperor Shen Nung, the discoverer of tea, wrote in his classic: 'Medicines of the highest type put the human body at ease and protract life so that people ascend and become gods in heaven, soar up and down in the air, and have all the spirits at their service.' Which is quite a lot to expect of any diet! And some of the recipes suggested by these ancients seem to be equally bizarre and unpalatable. Among them are:

Asparagus: This is recommended for its sedative effects, though these take hold only very slowly. But asparagus eaten for a hundred days, say the philosophers, will give people great strength and enable them to walk quickly.

Thistle: This makes men slim and able to bear great burdens along cliff edges.

Other parts of this exotic pharmacopoeia bestow even more startling abilities.

Recommending the searcher to look beneath the roots of a thousand-year-old dead tree, the sages say that there will be a man-shaped root beneath it. Cut it and blood will ooze out. Rub this on your feet and you will be able to walk on water or on your nose and streams will open before you, and you will become invisible.

If you take a thousand-year-old bat, dry it and turn it into powder which you then eat, you will live for 40,000 years.

Many substances not normally considered to be food when eaten will give occult powers or protection according to the writings of Ko Hung, a Taoist scholar who collected hitherto unrecorded secret teachings in a volume called the *Nei P'ien* which was published in 320 AD. Many of these substances are those which are culturally valuable anyway, such as gold, jade, precious stones and pearls. Jade, for example, can make a man light enough to fly. It can be dissolved in black rice wine, says Ko, then crystallized or turned into pills. Eat these for a year or more and you will not become wet when you step into streams nor burned when you step into fire. Sharp things will never cut you, nor poison make you ill. He records a blind man whose sight was restored by drinking powdered jade.

Cinnamon, adds Ko, can be liquefied by cooking it with onion juice and then sipped after being mixed with bamboo liquid. Take this for seven years and you will be able to walk on water and also become immortal. Many of these occult foods give immortality if taken for long periods of time according to instructions. In fact, Ko lists over 300 different things to eat or drink all of which can lead to immortality. A number of them also convey the power to summon what Ko delightfully calls the Travelling Canteen, which is something like an occult self-service device: fragrant foods served on plates of gold and in cups of gold, which glides up to the deserving, presumably just as hunger strikes.

In amongst all these somewhat exotic and perhaps fanciful recipes and prescriptions, there was also quite a lot of good commonsense – as there usually is in Chinese beliefs. For example, when discussing how the ordinary person may obtain lasting good health, with the possibility of longevity, Ko talks about the philosophy of health which a wise person should follow.

Wounding occurs when our thought is troubled with things for which we lack talent. Sadness, decrepitude, uneasiness and torment are wounds, as is also excessive joy. Constant covetousness wounds. Wasting time abed, drunkenness and its vomitings, lying down after a heavy meal, getting breathless from running – all these are wounds. When wounds have been accumulated to the point of exhaustion, death soon ensues.

Therefore, the prescription for nurturing life is this: do not walk too fast. Do not listen too intently. Do not look too long. Do not sit too long. Do not stay in bed until you get too weak. Dress before you get chilled. Lighten your dress before you get overheated. Eat only to satiety. Do not overdrink. Don't overwork or take too much ease.

Don't overemphasize any of the Five Savours when eating, for too much acidity harms the spleen; too much bitterness harms the lungs; too much acridity harms the liver; too much salt harms the heart; too much sugar harms the kidneys.

But, of course, all this wisdom about the body system and its nutritional needs does not stop at food. The Chinese have also evolved a ritualistic set of beliefs and customs around drink, especially one particular drink.

'The Chinese have a herb, out of which they press a delicate juice which serves them for drink instead of wine: it also preserves their health and frees them from those evils which the immoderate use of wine produces amongst us.' Thus said one Giovanni Betero in 1590 in the first, known reference made in the West to that delicate herb – tea. And his enthusiasm was more than endorsed by the Chinese themselves who had been congratulating themselves on the delights of their own native shrub long before any foreigners ever knew anything about it. In the eighth century AD, Lu Yu wrote a classical treatise on tea call *Cha Ching*, or the *Book of Tea*, in which he commented 'Tea tempers the spirit, calms and harmonizes the mind; it arouses thoughts and prevents drowsiness, lightens and refreshes the body and cleans the perceptive faculties.'

No one knows how the use of tea originated but, of course, there is a Chinese legend about it. The legendary Emperor Shen Nung, who was reputed to have lived about 5000 years ago, was sitting beneath a tree one day, waiting patiently for some water to boil. As he sat there, a few leaves drifted down from the tree and fell into the water. Moments later a delicious aroma arose from the boiling water and, intrigued by this, his Imperial Majesty sipped the result, pronounced his approval and – lo and behold – tea had been discovered. For the Emperor had sat himself down at the base of the *Ternstroemiaceae*, or tea plant.

The tea plant is a distant cousin of the camellia, with leathery green leaves which are shining and spear-shaped. The flowers are white with an explosion of yellow stamens and, left to themselves, these native inhabitants of China would happily soar to 50 ft high or more and could easily live for seventy years. Since that first legendary accident, the Chinese have taken the care and consumption of that aromatic herb very seriously and a whole body of tea lore has grown up around the tiny leaves which first drifted down into the Emperor's boiling cauldron. Some of these beliefs have been verified in this century by western medical science and others have not, but neither have they been disproved.

The tea we usually see today – those little curled-up dried leaves – is only the latest form in which we drink it. There have been others. Tea has only really been a drink used for general refreshment in the past 1500 years in China. Before that, it was largely regarded as a medicinal drink to be taken for health purposes and people would no more have drunk it to quench thirst than we drink cough mixture for its wonderful bouquet. It was the aristocracy who first acquired the taste for tea as a pleasant infusion and this happened during the Han Dynasty. Then the favourite was brick tea, which can still be obtained from certain parts of China. In this, the tea leaves are pressed together and dried into loosely packed bricks. Sometimes the bricks are round with holes in the centre, like unwieldy woolly doughnuts, and they are made in this way so that a number of them can be strung together on a rope or over a stick for easy transportation. Back in the days of friendlier relations between Russia and China, the Chinese used to export their brick tea across the border to the Russians who couldn't have enough of it. To infuse brick tea, a chunk of the tea is broken off and steeped in hot water to make the black strong brew which resulted from this process. Tibetan tea is also usually made into this form for easy carrying by the nomads wandering with their yaks. Tibetans, however, love to add salt and butter to their tea. They do not, contrary to popular legend, like their tea butter rancid. It is merely that their butter often does go rancid in the months of wandering far from the yak pastures and they have to make do with it.

In the more refined Sung Dynasty, aristocratic tastes

turned to powdered tea which they used to make by pouring on hot water and then whipping up the mixture with a small twig brush, thus producing the world's first expresso tea. This tea powder was usually made from green teas, not the black tea of brick fame. It was only after these fashions had faded that the dried leaf we would recognize today gradually became popular, and it was also during this time that ordinary people became aware that the aristocrats had the right idea when they took to tea. Hot tea became the common man's drink – not cold, since the Chinese believe that cold drinks are bad for the body system – although, in times of famine, even hot water would do. Among most Chinese today a drink of hot water alone is often considered to be a very acceptable refreshment, although westerners in Hong Kong and Singapore find this hard to believe.

These days, Chinese teas fall into three major categories: green, black and oolong, which are ways of describing the treatment processes rather than the varieties of plant. There are other names for the tea plant varieties. Black teas, which are the only ones grown in India and Sri Lanka, are those which have been allowed to ferment. Green teas have not fermented at all, and oolongs are partly fermented. Sometimes you will come across other colour names, such as red or white, but these too fit into the three basic process divisions. In China, the black teas are made from leaves dried in the sun on bamboo trays which are gently tossed from time to time, and the leaves rolled over. After a few hours, they are then fried in a red-hot frying pan called a *kuo* and finally the leaves are rolled into balls. This process is repeated several times causing enzymes to be released which oxidize the leaves and turn them black. This is the fermentation. Eventually, when fermentation is judged to have gone far enough, the black tea is dried in a basket over a bright red charcoal fire, which cuts short the process of fermentation by killing the enzymes. Green teas are similarly treated in the drying process, but the leaves are fired over charcoal immediately after picking which kills all the fermentation enzymes before they can get to work, so that the leaves dry into a greenish-grey colour. Oolong, which means 'black dragon', starts fermenting but the process is not allowed to continue. These leaves dry to a darkish brown colour.

All the Chinese teas, whatever their name, fit into one of these three categories and all so-called 'Indian' teas, which originally came from China anyway, are black teas. The black tea of Sri Lanka is all Orange Pekoe, which was brought from China to northern India and then re-exported to Sri Lanka when its coffee plantations were killed off by blight. So it is really only from China that the great range of teas can be obtained. Taiwan now grows its own, an imitation of the Chinese teas, and even Hong Kong has one tea plantation, although it is not very extensive.

According to tradition, tea is one of the seven essentials of the Chinese household, the other six being firewood, rice, oil, salt, soy sauce and vinegar. A number of social functions revolve around it. Visitors are greeted with tea and, when the time comes for them to go, they will be speeded on their way with another brewing. It is even possible that apologies can be made with a fresh brew of tea. It can seal a pact between enemies and in Hong Kong it is not unknown for Triad Society gangsters to arrange truces over tea in a tea-house. It is used to flavour dishes and is even offered to the dead in their graves. Several varieties of tea are commonly to be found in Chinese homes and in the tea-houses of Hong Kong, Taiwan, Singapore and China. These would probably include Ti Kuan Yin, White Peony, Bo Lai and Lung Ching, quite apart from the special types such as brick tea and flower teas.

The best of all – the champagne of Chinese teas – is reputed to be Lung Ching, or Dragon's Well tea. This is a young, unfermented green tea, supposed to be taken before and during meals. It comes from the beautiful countryside of Hangchow and was once grown only for the Emperors and even now is served on great occasions.

When Richard Nixon went on his first famous visit to Chairman Mao, he was given Dragon's Well tea. This tea, like young Beaujolais, is meant to be drunk within a year of being picked as it deteriorates with age. It can be extremely expensive, especially in a year of poor harvest. It awakens the taste buds and enhances the digestion, as well as soothing the throat.

Ti Kuan Yin, or Iron Goddess of Mercy tea, is so-called because of its colour (iron-greenish grey) and taste (divine). It comes from Fukien Province and is usually drunk in tiny eggcup-size bowls, often with Chiuchow food. The tea leaves are blended from a mixture of green and oolong teas. It is a bitter tasting drink which is considered particularly thirst-quenching and good for reviving tired spirits.

Bo Lai is the favourite of most Cantonese. It comes from Yunnan Province and only the golden tips of the leaf are used to make this richly robust tea. The Cantonese love to drink it with *dimsum*, the special little snacks and dumplings which make up breakfast in a restaurant. It is said to stimulate the appetite and help the digestion. It is also supposed to keep you thin if you drink it with food and it is believed to have antiseptic qualities. So much so, that in Hong Kong people wash their chopsticks and rice bowls in tea before using them.

White Peony tea is made of the finest young leaves, gently massaged by hand and then dried in the wind but never touched directly by sunlight. This is considered to be excellent for respiration and bronchitis.

The jasmine teas so beloved by foreigners are usually an inferior green tea disguised by the addition of flowers; other possible additions can be lychee flowers, chrysanthemum and even rose petals. Tea experts recommend that those who like flower tea should buy a good green tea, then add their own choice of flower.

The Chinese tea so treasured by generations of maiden aunts – Lapsang Souchong – is a rather spurious pretender. Despite the authentic-sounding name, no Chinese even knows it, let along drinks it. Lapsang Souchong means 'Mr Lapsang's mixture' and Mr Lapsang was merely a clever entrepreneur who bought up an anonymous mix of black teas and shipped it out as China's finest, and that early consignment became the brand name for the many tons of the stuff that followed it.

Pleasant though it is to drink tea, it is the health-giving qualities for which the Chinese most prize the brew and interestingly enough science supports those apparently folksy beliefs. Scientific analysis of tea confirms that it has some twenty amino acids, thirty polypeptide bodies, twelve sugars, six organic acids and as much as 5 per cent caffeine and theophylline. It also has fluoride, vitamin C and B complex, plus nicotinic acid (B3). Theophylline is an active ingredient in relaxing the bronchioles, as well as helping to produce urine and stomach acid and speeding up the heartbeat, which covers many of the functions with which folklore accredits tea.

And tea lore would be nothing without the established ritual of making the heady brew. This differs today very little from the wisdom distilled by Lu Yu twelve centuries ago. In his treatise, written in 780 AD, he says that tea must be sipped, never gulped, from a pure porcelain bowl after it has been brewed in an earthenware pot from specially collected water. The water, says Lu Yu, must come from a slow-flowing mountain stream, never from fast or falling water. A river would do, if it was far from human habitation, but well water was quite inferior. Presumably tap water would have been totally beyond the pale, even had Lu Yu been able to imagine such a thing. The water must be brought to the boil, 'leaping like breakers majestic' and a small measure of salt should be added. His treatise was centred around the four necessary qualities of good tea: vivacity, clearness, fragrance and *kan* (a liquorice-like flavour). Neither did he overlook the importance of the setting, for he recommended that good tea be sipped in a bamboo grove, on a small bridge near a painted boat, or in a pavilion surrounded by water-lilies in the company of beautiful concubines.

12. Triad societies

A great deal of nonsense has been written about Chinese secret societies, now commonly known as Triad Societies or Tongs. Far from being the mysteriously powerful organizations so beloved of the more lurid newspapers, Triad Societies are merely loosely linked gangs of criminals associated with illegal gambling, narcotics, vice and protection rackets. They batten off their own people in Chinese communities all over the world, knowing that their compatriots will be reluctant to act against them in any way. That is for the twofold reason that the Chinese in general greatly fear the violence of the Triads, and are extremely unwilling to have anything to do with officials, especially policemen.

It is of course, easy to overestimate the power of the societies. They work entirely among the Chinese who are often cut off from the surrounding community by race and language. It is impossible for a non-Chinese to penetrate the societies because his face would give him away and it is rare for the Chinese to be interested in becoming policemen in foreign communities. Most Chinese accept corruption, in the sense that they feel that it is regrettable but probably inevitable. To fight it is foolhardy and dangerous. Triad Societies are not so much part of the worldwide conspiracy of crime as local import-export agents dealing in illegalities.

Today's Triad Society members, also called Triads, are not much more than petty criminals with a particular penchant for wielding razor-sharp melon knives and kitchen choppers against those who displease them. It is frequently rumoured that some of the most highly placed members of Chinese communities are high ranking Triads, but this has not been proved. It is certainly true, for example, in Hong Kong that a number of members of the Royal Hong Kong Police Force are also Triads and heavily involved in illegal and corrupt practices, but it is not possible to estimate accurately just how numerous they are. The official estimates of Triad Society membership stands at around 37,000 in Hong Kong, though some less official claims make a case for there being as many as 100,000. Neither figure is provable.

With Chinese communities in general being as enclosed as they usually are, by language, culture and choice, it is fairly easy for them to have an established line of communication which crosses countries and even continents. It is this compactness of overseas communities that sometimes deceives casual observers into thinking that Triads are far more organized than they really are. In fact, the Triad Societies tend to be rather split by dialect, background and frequent internecine rivalries and international co-operation in any truly efficient way does not really exist. There are too many ambitious entrepreneurs in each society to make such unity a likely event.

It is, therefore, not today's Triad Societies which really interest us in this chapter but rather the legendary history of the founding of the societies. Looking at the early history and at the actual initiation rituals, it is possible to see many ceremonial and legendary links with the traditions of Freemasonry. Scholars think it very unlikely that Freemasonry has evolved from the Chinese secret societies, but suggest instead that in fact both the Brotherhood of Freemasons and the Triad Societies share a common ancestry in the most ancient mystery cults. After their common origin, possibly in what is now the Middle East, they have diverged considerably, but still share fragments of their teachings, as well as certain aspects of their rituals.

The first secret societies of China were composed of religious men who were seeking a way to salvation through mystical rituals. They were concerned, not so much with what was happening in this world, but with another world, either that of the supernatural or the journey of the soul towards salvation. Even today there are elements of this. The answers to why Triad Societies have now become synonymous with terror, illegality and corruption, while the Masons with whom their rituals have much in common have become associated with bourgeois good works, must be found in the communities from which each comes, rather than in the actual roots of each. Obviously, where secrecy and vows of loyalty are concerned, there is every possibility that corrupt practices may arise. Examples of this can be cited among the secret societies of Christian origin, such as the Knights Templar who were popularly rumoured to have become both corrupt and heretical. Even if corruption itself does not actually exist, the very secrecy with which mystical cults surround themselves can easily lead to false accusations of corruption which the societies cannot refute without breaking their vows of secrecy.

Long before the Triads arose in the seventeenth century, there were secret societies much earlier in Chinese history. Unfortunately, they appear to have retained their vows of secrecy only too well and there is little or no solid evidence left to illuminate their ancient pathways into mystery. This does not prove they did not exist, since all their teachings were anyway passed by word of mouth and supposed never to have been written down, except possibly in the most temporary form for immediate destruction after each ceremony had been completed. There were said to have been a number of mystery cults existing in China from its earliest history. They may have continued their connection with the mystery cults of the Middle East and Europe for centuries after their origins, in that the Chinese courts of 2000 years ago were not isolated from the outside world as China has been during the last four centuries. The Chinese had trade exchanges throughout the world and strangers were welcomed to the imperial court with their foreign customs and philosophies. In fact, much of what we know as Chinese culture now had its origins elsewhere. For example, Chinese medicine owes much to India, from which the martial arts also came.

The first open official references to such societies came in the seventeenth century when the Emperor Kian Hsi, the second Manchu ruler, issued an edict condemning certain Taoist secret societies. These Taoist societies were the continuers of the mystery cults which had taken on the trappings of Taoism as the Freemasons have taken on the trappings of Christianity. The societies named by the Emperor included the Society of the White Lily, the Hung Society, the Incense Burners, the Origin of Chaos and the Origin of the Dragon. We do not know what those societies were, and neither probably did the Emperor who did not very much like the threat of their secrecy. Scholars make a connection between the White Lily and the Hung Society, but do not know if one led to the other or if they were actually one and the same. Certainly the Hung Society is one of the names of the Triad Societies, but whether Triad rituals come from the White Lily Society is not known.

It is, of course, very unsatisfactory that we do not possess more detailed information about the societies but, if it comes to that, we know very little about the central mysteries of the Greek mystery cults either. Possibly the answers to both mysteries would be the same.

We do have some early information about certain historical events which refer to the White Lily Society. In the fifth century AD, the leader of the White Lily Society was a Buddhist teacher called Eon or Hwui-yin. Some scholars claim that the White Lily Society was founded at this time, but it seems more likely that it was then that the society became heavily influenced by the Buddhism which had newly arrived in China. That it was already an ecstasy cult became obvious under the leadership of Eon who set up a Buddhist community which meditated upon the teachings and name of the Buddha. Most mystery cults are deeply involved with the death journey and what happens as a living soul passes through the gates of death, whether this is then taken merely as an allegory or as a preparation for the actuality of death or whether, perhaps, a death sacrifice was involved. Certainly Eon's cultists were faithful to this pattern. His followers underwent some kind of mystical initiation and a central tenet of their faith was the belief that they would go to the Western Paradise, the place of afterlife for Buddhists who were freed from the wheel of reincarnation either temporarily or throughout eternity.

After about 600 AD, members of the society were persecuted, initially for their Buddhism and then perhaps for their secrecy. No further written references to the society appear for another 700 years, during which time we must assume that its rituals continued but its members avoided all political interference and concentrated on mystical matters.

The society obtained some additional notoriety around 1344 AD when its leader, then Han Shan-tung, led a rebellion against Mongol invaders. He had four companions in this venture and they distinguished themselves by wearing red headbands or turbans, becoming known as the Red Turban Rebels. There are some scholars who see a distinct connection between this first five and the Five Ancestors of the later Triad legends.

It was the very secrecy of these societies which has

made it difficult for historians to trace the direct line of
events linked with them. It was quite common for such
societies to change their names and a number of designa-
tions may all in fact refer to what are now known as Triad
Societies. For example, during its official condemnation
in the reigns of the first two Ching Emperors, we know
that the Society of the White Lily later became the Society
of the White Lotus. There is also a reference in the edict to
the *T'in Tei Hui* (the Society of Heaven and Earth) which
is still the name of the Triad Societies. These references
may all be to one society – we simply do not know.

Meanwhile, the Triad Societies themselves have a
traditional mythology which usually forms part of the
initiation ritual. Triad, by the way, is not a translation
from the Chinese. It is an English term for the Hung
Society. The Chinese character *Hung*, enclosed by a
triangle, represents the union of Heaven, Earth and Man
– the three which make up the Triad. The character
Hung, as is usual with the Chinese language, has a
number of connotations. It is said to refer to the founder
of the Ming Dynasty, the patriot Hung Wu, and also has
connotations of red. The first meeting of the first Triad
Society was said to have taken place in the Red Flower
Pavilion and an early auspicious sign was the sudden
reddening of the sky, and so on. The society is also
commonly known as the Three United Association,
with the same theme as Triad, and in Hong Kong they
are simply known as *Hak Sha Ui*, or Black Societies,
because of their criminality.

It is popularly said that Triad Societies date from the
seventeenth century AD, when they were set up as secret
political organizations to overthrow the Mongolian
conquerors who had seized the Dragon Throne and set
themselves up as the Ching Emperors. The aim of the
secret societies of that time was to take China back under
Chinese rule and drive out the hated invaders. However,
scholars disagree with this interpretation. Instead, they
claim that the comparatively modern founding of the
Triad Societies was actually a revitalization or politiciz-

ing of much older secret societies with completely different aims. Triad Society members encountered much imperial oppression and were therefore forced to develop secret signs, passwords and symbols by which they could recognize each other and yet remain safe and undetected among strangers. The oppression also led to emigration and the carrying of Triad power overseas, to the United States where they have frequently been referred to as the Tongs, and to any place where the Chinese have settled in large numbers.

It is said that a rebellion against the usurping Ching Emperors broke out in Szechuan Province and was brutally put down by Ching soldiers. The rebels were mostly killed and a few survivors took refuge in the Siu Lam, or Shaolin, Monastery which has been variously placed in Hunan and Fukien Province. There the survivors hid out and continued their military training, ready to rise again as soon as they had gathered enough followers. The martial monks of Shaolin are also, incidentally, regarded as the holy fathers of *kung fu*, the rough street-fighting martial art which has been so popularized in rather bad films from Hong Kong in recent years.

The story becomes rather complex at this stage. The traditional history claims that these rebellious military monks in fact helped out the Ching Emperors during a threatened invasion by outsiders and were greatly rewarded. Imperial favour did not smile upon them for long, however, and finally the Emperor sent soldiers to burn down the templeful of martial artists. There were then 128 monks in residence and they were betrayed by the seventh monk, Ma Ling Yee. 110 perished in the flames. The surviving eighteen fled and thirteen were killed during pursuit, leaving five left alive. These five managed to cross a river by means of a straw sandal, which turned into a boat just in time to save them, and they became the Five Ancestors of the first Triad Societies. A lot of further adventures befell the Five Ancestors and from these legendary adventures comes much of the esoteric language of the initiation ritual, or so the Triads claim but scholars say this is merely a much later rationalization of early mystery rituals preserved but not understood by those who used them. They then introduced a new legendary structure to try to simplify the rituals which they no longer comprehended.

The Five Ancestors set up Five Lodges all over China. These were as follows:

1st Lodge: The Green Lotus Hall of Phoenix District, which is said to cover Fukien and Kansu Provinces. In fact, as these two provinces are widely separated at opposite corners of China, some scholars suggest that Kansu is a mistranscription for Kiangsi, which would be geographically more logical.

2nd Lodge: Hung Obedience Hall of the Golden Orchid District of Kwangtung and Kwangsi Provinces; the Lodge of Hong Kong Triad Societies.

3rd Lodge: Heavenly Queen Hall of the Happy Border District of Yunnan and Szechuan Provinces.

4th Lodge: Great Blending Hall of the Beautiful Lotus District, covering Hunan and Hupei Provinces.

5th Lodge: Extensive Conversion Hall of the Western Dyke District, over Chekiang, Kiangsi (but perhaps this should be Kansu), and Honan Provinces.

The intention of the Five Ancestors was to raise a country-wide rebellion against the Manchu Emperors who had seized the Imperial Dragon Throne, but this never really materialized. There were individual revolts throughout the country but nothing of significant size. The first really major uprising, ironically enough, was that encouraged by the fearsome Dowager Empress herself. The Boxer Rebellion of 1900 was not entirely a Triad venture, but it is believed that a number of the Boxers were Triad Society members. Certainly some of the Boxers' beliefs – that they were divinely possessed and could not be injured or killed – do carry through into certain of the Triad-linked martial arts, some of which are thought to give invincibility to those who practise them. This, however, is really an offshoot of beliefs about spirit possession rather than part of the mainstream of Triad activities.

In China, as the movement towards republicanism grew, Doctor Sun Yat-sen himself approached the Triad Societies for political help. He is said to have been a high-ranking Triad Society official himself, who worked in both Honolulu and Chicago as a fighter official. Although Sun's organization was illegal, it was considered to be largely political, similar to the original revival of the secret societies' aims in the seventeenth century. However, he also approached many of the largely criminal societies for political support, promising them a role in the new China when the Emperors were driven out and the people took over.

He stood by this, once his revolution had succeeded in overthrowing the Manchus, and the Triad Societies rose to great social prominence in the new China. Even though their avowed aim at foundation – to free China from foreign rule – had been achieved, they were not content to have freed China for the Chinese. Instead, they attained great political power, became extremely corrupt and gradually degenerated into the totally criminal organizations of today.

In Hong Kong the Triad Societies have a very special history, partly because of the way in which they have dominated many aspects of life for ordinary people – a role which continues even today, unfortunately. It is also largely from Hong Kong that the Triads of recent years – those which spattered the streets of San Francisco with blood, have been involved in bombing and arson in London's Soho and puts gangs of youths at each others' throats in Vancouver – have spread all over the world, bringing disgrace on the many hard working members of the Chinese community trying to make new lives overseas.

Despite the founding of the 2nd Lodge in Kwangtung and Kwangsi Provinces, it is believed that Hong Kong very early on became its actual headquarters. Hong Kong was only founded in 1841 and already, by 1845, a government ordinance to outlaw the Triad Societies had been passed. One of the provisions of this hard-hitting ordinance was that Triads should be branded on the face after conviction, but this caused an outcry in the slightly more liberal Houses of Parliament and convicted Triad Society members were thereafter branded on the arm. Estimates at the time suggested that three-quarters of the Chinese population of Hong Kong were members of such societies.

In the middle years of the century, the Triad Societies dug deep into the areas where they still dominate today. They extorted money from labourers and street hawkers, which is still common in Hong Kong. They also penetrated the police force, which is likewise not unusual now in Hong Kong, as any perusal of the court proceedings in the daily newspapers will reveal. In the first half of the twentieth century, the Triads were fairly strictly controlled by their officials and open riots or even gang fights became rather rare. They were well-ensconced in the population, often working through guilds and trade unions but were considered to be quite well-behaved – just a regular quiet extortion racket to keep the coffers full. The Chinese have been accustomed to having to pay off someone throughout their long history – imperial officials, the police, tax collectors – and they do not really react very strongly to the continuance of the practice. Not that they condone it, but they feel helpless to protest.

During the Second World War, while the colony was under Japanese occupation, the Triad Societies showed their concern for their fellow Chinese who were suffering hunger, deprivation and summary execution in the streets by opening brothels and gambling dens for the Japanese officers. During these years, which were fat ones for the Triads, the Wo group of Triads were able to secure their domination of the colony, which was to stand them in good stead after the war was over.

After the Communists took over China, the Triad

strength in Hong Kong was greatly increased by the sudden exodus of those who had been involved in criminal activities in the mainland. In the early fifties, Triad power continued to rise until the riots of October 1956, during which the Triads took advantage of the general unrest and disorder to indulge in looting and crime. Because of this, the Triad Bureau was set up by the Royal Hong Kong Police Force and in the four years following its foundation some 10,000 Triads were arrested and prosecuted, while another 500 were thrown out of the colony. Since that time, it is questionable how much Triad activity has really declined, but it certainly seems to be true that the centralized organization has gone. Now it is every man for himself, and this tends to lead to the outbreaks of violence which characterize these gangster types both in Hong Kong and in most Chinese communities overseas.

There have been a great many other incidents of Triad interaction in the last twenty years, but that belongs in a different book. One interesting point, though, is that most so-called Triads today have probably not been initiated according to the full rituals. That is certainly true in Hong Kong, where initiations have become more crude and incomplete year by year. It is probably not so true in, for example, Taiwan, where traditions remain and where, in fact, Triad Societies are not illegal. Instead, like the Masons, they have their lodges where they meet regularly and they certainly still use the full ritual with all its mystical elements.

Whether or not the members are initiated by full ritual – without which, by the way, they cannot be considered true Triads – they all tend to use the same terminology for ranks.

Triad Ranks: All are designated by names and by numbers which indicate their inner meaning by the elaborate punning which is only possible in a language with the numerous tones that Chinese can have. While even Mandarin, or Peking dialect, is open to this with its four tones, Cantonese has up to nine tones.

489 or First Route Marshal: Head of the Triad branch, also known as Mountain Lord.

438 or Second Route Marshal: Deputy head of a branch and also known as Assistant Mountain Lord. This title goes as well to the Vanguard or Incense Master, both of whom officiate at ceremonies.

415 or White Paper Fan: Advisor on administration, finance and organization of the branch.

426 or Red Pole: Head fighter and battle strategist.

432 or Straw Sandal: Liaison and messenger. He communicates with branch members and is responsible for organizing battles and meetings with other societies. He also delivers demand notes when necessary, for ransom or protection money.

49: A low-rank initiate, usually fee-paying and under the protection of an officer.

These numbers are not necessarily always used. For example, a branch head does not always assume the number 489. The number is used only by a very experienced official who has been elected to his post and there could even be several bearers of this number in a branch of a Triad Society if their experience and excellence – in gangster terms, of course – merited it.

The significance of these numbers is explained in the Triad history, but in fact it is far more likely that they have direct links with ancient mystery rites from which Triad Societies have degenerated, as numerology was a major part of Chinese occultism. The Triad explanations are linked with the more recent Triad history, which has obviously been invented in order to give a rational explanation to a long-established and no longer understood tradition.

However, according to the Triad history, the numbers represent the following mythology. The figure four which precedes all ranks is said to represent the four seas which the Chinese believed surrounded the earth, and stands for the universe. It also contains a punning reference to the Chinese quotation 'We are brothers within the Four Seas'.

The leader's number, 489, is broken down in the following way:4 + 8 + 9 = 21 and the Chinese character for twenty-one echoes the character for Hung, the Hung Society name. In 438, the four is set aside, leaving three and eight which combine in written Chinese to refer to the character for the Hung Society. 426 is broken down into 4 × 26 + 4 = 108, the number of the legendary heroes of the Sung Dynasty who fought against imperial tyranny. It is also a common mystical number throughout the East; there are 108 mudras in Indian traditional dance, and so on. 415 is broken down into 4 × 15 +4 = 64, the number of hexagrams in the *I-Ching* or *Book of Changes*. 432 breaks into 4 × 32 = 128 which is said to have been the number of patriots who practised martial arts in the Siu Lam, or Shaolin, Monastery. The name Straw Sandal is said to refer to the miraculous straw sandal which turned into a boat and carried some of the Shaolin monks to safety when they were being pursued by enemies. Forty-nine breaks down into 4 × 9 = 36, the number of vows the initiate must take, also a mystical number.

All of which seems a little far-fetched in that the numbers have to be heavily manipulated to bring them into the explanations given. At one time, it is quite obvious the numbers and their usage were linked to religious or magical rites, which were an intrinsic part of Chinese mysticism very early on, as they were part of the Kabbalistic system of mystical knowledge too. All communities, no matter how sophisticated, retain particles and fragments of these beliefs in the power of the number – witness, the unlucky thirteen of Europe and the United States. The very idea of not calling a floor on a building thirteen is ridiculous and yet that is standard practice in the sophisticated America of today. Therefore, it is even more likely that a civilization that has kept more fully in touch with its ancient teachings, like China, will have retained powerful numerological influences.

The mere fact that the Triad members themselves may not know the inner meaning of the numerology themselves proves nothing. Most people who feel that way about the number thirteen have no idea of the origin of the superstition either.

The Triad initiation ritual is fascinating in that it is really the Chinese Book of the Dead. Like the Tibetan Book of the Dead, and the Freemason's ritual, it is the enactment of the journey of a soul into death, through the gates of death and into the world beyond, perhaps to reincarnation or perhaps to paradise. That is probably not the way the Triads themselves view it, For them, it is merely, but also importantly, a binding by a death oath into the secrets of the Hung Society. No man, once he has taken part in the initiation ritual, can ever cease to be a Triad. He is a Triad until death and death is the payment for those who do try to leave.

Initiations vary greatly in detail, although they all have rituals and references in common. When they appear in different places – such as Malaysia or Hong Kong – their actual format also differs. The reason for this is fairly obvious. All Triad teachings were part of the ancient mysteries handed down through the centuries by way of an oral tradition alone. As I have mentioned, they were never supposed to be written down, except hastily for individual rituals. There have been occasions when police or official intervention broke up a ritual before its completion and it is from these that the written ritual procedure has been obtained. It did not happen often – one official's specific duty during rituals was to keep an eye on the writings and, if any interruption indicated the danger of intruders, to destroy them instantly by burning them.

Inevitably, when an oral tradition comes down through the centuries and is often passed on by men who do not, in fact, understand their inner meaning, changes must occur. Even in something as simple as the children's party game when a whispered message is passed around a circle, a simple sentence such as 'John has seven boxes' can turn into a garbled, 'John has smelly socks'. Such confusion is vastly multiplied when the time of passing is not minutes but centuries and a complex and involved ritual is concerned. A double confusion arises because the more recent history of the Triad Societies – invented almost to explain the now incomprehensible references – now overlies the original teachings. Therefore, what stands now as the Triad initiation is just the fragmentary remainder left over from the ancient mystical tradition of the secret cults.

The initiate starts out on his mystical journey from the East, the place of dawn in which the divine merges with the material. He answers a series of questions from the Incense Master which serve as his identification, describing how he came to be at the Lodge. These are not literal questions, but metaphorical ones and the answers are based upon the foundations of Chinese culture – the structure of the soul, the bonds of the community, the form of the afterlife according to Chinese belief. He also refers to the Eight Immortals of Chinese mythology and other figures from the Chinese pantheon of heroes, deities and historical beings. All of this exchange serves to root the ritual deep into the accepted culture of the Chinese. It is almost a summing-up of the mutual reference points from which the members of the Triad Society come. As the words are supposed to be memorized by the initiate, they may well constitute an education as well as a way of unifying the Lodges from all over China by ensuring that they share a common mythology and cultural experience. Given the very wide variety of tribes and ethnic groups in the vastness of China, it is a doubly unifying teaching.

The rituals contain many references to the old fertility cults and nature worship which still underlie many of the practices of Chinese villagers in Taiwan, Hong Kong and mainland China. The ritual journey causes the initiate to cross sacred mountains – which appear in many such ancient rites, for example among the Babylonians – to sail on a mystical ship, similar to certain references in the

Tibetan Book of the Dead – to encounter many of the heroes of Chinese culture. Not surprisingly, many Buddhist references occur, but these are likely to be an addition from the days of the Buddhist conversion of China when the secret societies became very involved with mystical Buddhism.

The initiate continues under interrogation to describe the wonders and the puzzles that he sees on his journey. He sees a wondrous ship in the prow of which stands the Queen of Heaven – the Chinese goddess Kwan Yin, a figure strangely similar to the Virgin Mary in Christian tradition – and he sets sail on the ship in the company of deities who protect him. The great ship sails to the underworld and comes eventually to the island of the blest, on which stands a bridge guarded by souls of the dead and the Buddhas. This bridge – similar to the Brig o' Dread of early Christian ballad in England – is watched over by an old man selling magical fruit from a stall. The initiate passes the bridge and this is probably the point at which he is regarded as actually initiated, entering the mystical brotherhood.

Passing through a great hall thronged with people, he comes to the Circle of Heaven and Earth in which he finds a holy city, the City of Willows, surrounded by five double walls inscribed with verse. He continues to tell of what he sees in the holy city, coming to the corpse of a dead man with his legs crossed. This is said to be the traitor monk, A' T'sat, who betrayed the Siu Lam monks, but as the word *t'sat* means both seven and death it could represent the death of the earthly part of the initiate now that he has entered the brotherhood. The brother then passes through the West Gate and comes upon a fiery mountain guarded by a spirit and beyond that comes again to the very simple temple in which his initiation is taking place.

The newly welcomed brother is then introduced to the other members in the temple, named the Red Flower Pavilion after the legendary first meeting of the first Triad Society. Outside the temple stand the sun and the moon. He then tells the Incense Master that he has been reborn. He summarizes the journey he has just been through symbolically and then takes the Thirty-Six Oaths which bind him to observe all the rules of the society or die.

While this initiation is very near to the classical ritual of the ancient societies, it may very greatly today. In Hong Kong, for example, the ritual has many more very direct references to the seventeenth-century Triad mythology, which is certainly a reasonably modern overlay. There is no doubt at all that for most of the young thugs joining Triad Societies now, the mystical significance of the old ritual is totally meaningless. And even though Triads still take the Thirty-Six Oaths, they seem to make very little effort to abide by them, even in their dealings with others of their own particular branch of the society. The only possible reason why any of the ritual is still used is merely to try to make an impression strong enough to act as a form of discipline on the new young members; and that it patently does not do.

It may well be that the purely mystical secret societies do still exist, although they may have very few members. Certainly during my enquiries undertaken in the research of this book, I was assured that there are still mystical associations existing, even in China itself, and that these still pursue the great work of following the Path of Light. They would seem to have a great deal in common with their spiritual brothers the Freemasons, the Rosicrucians, the Kabbalists and other groups known to be involved with the search for spiritual power. The criminal Triad Societies are an unfortunate example of what happens when a spiritual organization becomes corrupted by the search for material power.

Like the Masons, Triad Society brothers can identify each other even as strangers among strangers, through hand signals of a reasonably discreet nature, through ways of handling ordinary everyday objects and through special slang. For example, a general pass sign used to be the right hand outstretched with all five fingers apart.

Another sign could be the touching of the middle finger of the right hand with the thumb and so on. The Triads can also use a secret sign language which is somewhat like the sign language used by the deaf and through which quite lengthy conversations can take place. These days we would hardly see the point of that, but in the days when Triad Society members came from all over China and might well not have shared a mutual dialect, it obviously served a useful purpose in enabling conversation to take place.

Scholars think that the sign language has very ancient origins indeed. The Indians of North America, for example, had a very complex sign language which enabled members of different tribes to talk without sharing a spoken language. As they too are Mongol in origin, like the Chinese, it suggests that the use of sign language goes back to their common ancestry. In Hong Kong, the officials of the 2nd Lodge, the Triad Lodge of Hong Kong, use particular signals to identify themselves. Unfortunately, Triads have become so sloppy in the last two or three decades that such officials not uncommonly use the wrong signals for their rank – which is why most experts think that what passes for Triad lore among the Cantonese is not to be taken as very authentic any more.

The use of Triad slang was once a form of secret password which could be slipped into ordinary conversation but which enabled brothers to identify each other discreetly and thus to signal their allegiance. It may well still serve that purpose in some parts of the world, but in Hong Kong, Triad slang has become so commonly used that the government ordinance outlining the setting up of radio and television services has had to include a total ban on the use of Triad language in the spoken media.

The kind of slang which might be Triad language is very extensive indeed and it changes all the time. After all, slang which is public knowledge can hardly be of much use in enabling members of secret societies to identify each other. Some obsolete examples of Triad slang are:

Triad	Meaning
A draught of wind	A spy, a policeman
A horse	A man
Melon seeds	Money
A lantern	An eye
Chasing the dragon	To smoke heroin

The last phrase has passed into such common usage that it is even used in the West now by heroin addicts or law officers to describe heroin smoking, but it started out as Triad slang.

The Thirty-Six Oaths, of which mention has been made several times, tend to vary from society to society but in general their terms of reference are similar in that they aim to curb the lawless instincts of these common gangsters, at least in as far as their behaviour to each other is concerned. Of course, they do not actually do so and some would think it rather ridiculous anyway to imagine that organized gangs of thugs would be likely to observe a gentlemanly code of etiquette even amongst themselves but, be that as it may, the taking of the oaths is a still vital part of the process of initiation. Even in Hong Kong, where most of the once-elaborate ceremonial has been cut down to real hole-in-the-corner mutterings, new young Triads do have to take the oaths.

1 A brother must honour his parents and his brothers [most references to 'brothers' refer to other members of the Triad Society therefore, blood brothers] and if he breaks this law, he shall be drowned within one month in the Great Sea and his flesh and bones will be separated.

2 A brother must not envy what his brother has nor try to get it from him by deceit. If he breaks this law, may he be hung.

3 A brother must not impose on the weak nor quarrel with his brothers because of his wife. If he breaks this law, may he be struck by five lightning bolts or die the death of a thousand cuts and his bones be scattered

[which would be dire indeed for the rest of his family as his ghost would have no resting place].

4   A brother must not bring disrepute upon his brotherhood [which is patently laughable when the average Triad Society activities are considered]. If he breaks this law, may he be hung.

5   A brother must not harm his brothers. If he breaks this law, may he die the death of a thousand cuts.

6   A brother must not seduce the wife of a brother. If he breaks this law, may he be drowned in the Great Sea.

7   A brother must obey the laws laid down by his ancestors, neither may he become an officer before the proper time. If he breaks this law, may he be poisoned.

8   Brothers must not quarrel over male or female prostitutes. If this law is broken, may the brother be chopped into a thousand pieces.

9   No brother may interrupt a ceremony or walk in or out of the Lodge during a ceremony. If this law is broken, may he be struck by five lightning bolts and his blood gush forth.

10   No brother may scorn the hospitality of another brother or refuse to eat in his house. If he breaks this law, may he die in the streets like a beggar.

11   A brother may not write harmful letters about other brothers. If he breaks this law, may he die by the knife and his body be scattered.

12   A brother must not take the side of his own brother against his brothers in the Triad Society. If he breaks this law, may he be drowned in the Great Sea.

13   A brother must be served tea and rice when he enters the house of another brother. If this law is broken, may the offending brother bleed to death in the street.

14   A brother must not steal his brother's money. If he breaks this law, may he die the death of a thousand cuts or be eaten by a tiger.

15   If a brother's family is in need, another brother must

help them. If he breaks this law, may he bleed to death in the street.

16   If a brother who is taking care of another brother's household or possessions allows them to be stolen away, may he be struck dead by bolts of lightning and his bones scattered.

17   A brother may not marry the widow of another brother. If he breaks this law, may he be struck dead by five lightning bolts and his bones scattered.

18   A brother must lay aside any blood feuds he had with other brothers once he enters the society. If he breaks this law, may he be drowned in the Great Sea.

19   If a brother is asked for travelling money by another brother, he must pay him. If he breaks this law, may he die in the street.

20   If a brother gives away the secret ceremonies of the society, may he be eaten by a tiger or have his eyes bitten out by a snake.

21   If a brother takes money from another brother by false pretences, may he be drowned in the Great Sea.

22   If a brother fails to hand on money given him by another brother for that brother's family, may he be struck by arrows and knives.

23   If a brother borrows money from another brother and does not pay it back, may he be hung.

24   If a brother starts a street riot, and refuses to listen to warnings, may he die of poison.

25   If a brother cheats another brother, may he be struck by lightning.

26   If a brother causes trouble by slander within the society, may he die the death of a thousand cuts.

27   If a brother travelling from far comes to another brother's house, he must be received kindly and given hospitality. If this law is broken, may he bleed to death in the street.

28   May a brother who deliberately goes about and

causes trouble die in misery.

29   If a brother withholds information from the society which he has been given by another brother, may he bleed to death in the street.

30   If a brother is away, it is the duty of another brother to watch his wife and to punish any with whom she commits adultery. If he breaks this law, may he be eaten by a tiger.

31   If a brother is arrested, he must not implicate any other brothers. If he breaks this law, may he drown in the Great Sea and his descendants for a hundred generations live in misery.

32   If a brother dies and leaves a wife and children behind, if any other brother try to oppress her in any way, may he vomit forth all his blood.

33   If a brother does not always obey his parents, he shall be struck by lightning.

34   If a brother introduces into the society anyone who wants to discover its secrets, he shall be punished by seventy-two blows from the Red Pole.

35   If a brother learns that the government is seeking one of his brothers for arrest, he will help him to escape. If he breaks this law, may he be drowned in the Great Sea.

36   After he enters the society, a brother shall be loyal and faithful and keep as his purpose the overthrow of Ching and the restoration of Ming and keep as his common purpose with his brothers the aim to avenge the Five Ancestors.

Bearing in mind the kind of work which Triad Society members do – murder, maiming, protection and extortion rackets, drug dealing, prostitution, illegal gambling, gang-fighting, rape, theft – many people might find the above vows somewhat risible. But then this paradox of nobility and corruption is very much at the centre of the whole Triad tradition, one which began many centuries ago with the highest motive towards spiritual growth and which has been slowly bleeding to death in a gutter throughout this century.

Appendix:
Chinese deities

The following deities are among the most common to feature in the temples and on the family altars of the Chinese.

Guan Di (also known as Guan Gung and Mo) He is the God of Martial Arts and War and was said to be a real person born as Guan Yu in 160 AD. He is supposed to protect people from the ravages of war and has always been a favourite of the Chinese, for a very obvious reason. Interestingly, he is much-honoured by the criminal elements of the Cantonese who seem to feel an affinity for him. And of course the police like him too, perhaps for the same reason. He is the god most commonly found in police stations and brothels throughout Hong Kong and among the Cantonese of American and Britain.

Tin Hau The Goddess of the Sea, beloved of the fishing people, also said to have been a real person, a young girl who showed great ability to forecast the weather and who was deified after death. Many deities were humans first. Also known as Ma Ku and the Queen of Heaven.

Guan Yin The Buddhist Goddess of Mercy, a sinofied version of a deity from Tibetan Mahayana Buddhism. Originally a male incarnation who mysteriously changed sex early on during his adoption by the Chinese.

Tu Di The Earth Gods of a particular locality.

Monkey (also known wrongly as the Monkey God by westerners, and honoured by the title Great Saint Equal with Heaven by the Chinese) This is the hero of the great Chinese novel *A Record of the Journey to the West* also translated as *Monkey*. The book, which tells of the bringing of Buddhist scriptures to China from India, is a collection of incidents based upon popular folksongs, folktales and anecdotes about gods, ghosts and heroes current at the time of writing (about the sixteenth century AD). It is possibly the rough equivalent of Bunyan's *Pilgrim's Progress* but with a light, humorous touch not found in Bunyan.

Saam Dai Chu (also known as the Third Prince) He was the third son of a general in the twelfth century BC, named No-cha Li, who committed suicide to save his family from disgrace. He is considered to be Guan Yin's assistant and holds the position of Prime Minister of Heaven. He has many devotees in Singapore.

Jade Emperor A Taoist dignitary who is one of the highest deities of the Taoist pantheon.

Eight Immortals These are all Taoist dignitaries and they often appear in temples and on religious scrolls. They are Chao Kuo-Chin, the patron of mummers and actors; Lan Chai-ho, the patron of gardeners and florists; Lu Tung-pin, the patron of the sick; Chang Kuo-lao, the patron of artists and scribes; Han Shang-chu, the patron of musicians; Ho Hsien-ku, the patron of housewifery; Chung Li-chuan, the patron of the discoverers of the Elixir of Life and Li T'ieh Kuai, the patron of astrologers and magicians. These are very likely to be found in the business places of the relevant trades and professions.

Shakyamuni The name given to the Buddha in Tibetan Mahayana Buddhism.

Maitreya The Buddha who is yet to come, also known as the Buddha of the Future.

Eighteen Lohan The eighteen disciples of the Buddha.

Lao Tzu The founder of the Taoist doctrine.

Lo Pan The god of carpenters. As wood was commonly used for building in China rather than stone, the carpenters were more important than the masons.

Further reading

Dore, Henry *Researches into Chinese Superstitions*. Tusewei
    Printing Press, Shanghai, 1917.
Elliott, Alan J.A.*Chinese Spirit Medium Cults in Singapore*.
    L.S.E., London, 1955.
Encyclopedia Sinica. Published by Kelley and Walsh, Shan-
    ghai, 1917.
Groot. J.J.M. de *The Religious System of China*. Brill, Leyden,
    1901.
Morgan, W.P. *Triad Societies in Hong Kong*. Government
    Printer, Hong Kong, 1960.
Ward, J.S.M. *The Hung Society*. A. Lewis, Shepperton 1925.

And, for a comprehensive introduction to the Chinese, the
    reader could not do better than to read David Bonavia's
    elegant and entertaining *The Chinese*, Penguin Books, Lon-
    don 1981.